Fenway Pole Finder

FENWAY POLE FINDER

and Boston Baseball Fan Guide

Tim Shea

Itasca Books
Minneapolis, Minnesota

For information about this book or to contact the publisher, go to fenwaypolefinder.com

Cover illustration by Christine Esposito
Photos by Tim Shea

The text is set in Goudy Old Style and Arial.

Published by Itasca Books, Minneapolis, Minnesota
Printed in the United States of America
First printing, July 2006

10 9 8 7 6 5 4 3 2 1

Library of Congress Cataloguing-in-Publication data has been applied for.

ISBN 0-9767054-7-8

Contents

6
7
SAVE FENWAY PARK !
WE'RE #1
BOSTON
RED SOX

Introduction

Be they friend or foe of The Nation, any fan who experiences a Sox game at Fenway immediately knows they are enjoying the greatest park ever to grace the baseball landscape. The wonderfully inexplicable outfield dimensions, the fabled Green Monster, and the positively palpable scent of history tells the visitor that this certainly is the most glorious baseball home every built, added on to, renovated, and reinvigorated.

Opened in 1912, Fenway has been a second home to New England baseball fans for almost a century. In the late 1990s, the caretaker owners devised a plan to build a new "Fenway Park" adjacent to the real Fenway Park. They said renovation would be too costly and impractical, and they wanted to improve the ballgame experience for all fans, by giving them access to better amenities and more comfortable seats.

Thankfully, the ownership group that purchased the team for $700 million in 2002 had the foresight and decency to discard any notions of a new Fenway. Incrementally over the past four years, the new owners have done a superb job renovating and enhancing the fan experience through a variety of improvements. Adding the famous Green Monster seats and right field roof restaurant are two of the most dramatic additions, but there have been countless other subtle and creative changes, including greatly improving the variety and quality of food available, and clearing out storage areas to increase the public areas away from the seating.

More than ever, Fenway is now a baseball paradise. It is a destination unto itself, and the fact that the home team is consistently good only adds to the enjoyment. The food and beverage options have been multiplied and enhanced to suit every taste. The improvements also extend beyond the walls of Fenway itself, as even the famous Cask'n'Flagon, once mainly a spot to grab a cold one before, after, or instead of, a game, now smacks of gentility with its dining tables on a veranda that look out upon the back of the Monster.

While the improvements to the park over the past several years have astounded all observers, there is one lingering element that may be beyond the team's control: the infamous poles. Needed to support the park's second level, which now includes the press box, luxury boxes, pavilion seating, and the tony new EMC Club, the poles at Fenway are legendary for their ability to make you move backward, forward, and sideways in your seat so you don't miss key moments of the action.

There are many different types of seats at Fenway: Field Box, Loge Box, Outfield Box, Grandstand, Bleachers, Green Monster seats, Right Field Roof Box seats, and more. However, it is only the Grandstand Seats that have poles between the fans and the action on the field. Since most of the box seats are owned by season ticket holders, the average fan most often finds himself buying Grandstand or Bleacher seats. Some of the seats that are located behind poles are marked Obstructed View; others may not be.

In addition to providing useful information about how to get the most out of your Fenway experience, this book will help you identify those seats that have a pole impeding the view of home plate or the pitcher's mound, which is where the average fan's attention is focused during the majority of a game. Some fans may be surprised to learn that only about 3 percent of all the Grandstand seats have pole issues. That statistic, however, is not likely to be very comforting to the fans sitting behind a pole.

Some Facts about the Poles

- There are 26 poles positioned between the loge box seats (red) and grandstand seats (blue).
- Each steel pole is painted green and is approximately 16 inches wide.
- The poles are evenly spaced around the park, from sections 1 to 33.

How to Get Tickets

Having a great time at Fenway is a very easy thing to do. Getting tickets to the game you want to see, however, can be very difficult, frustrating, or expensive. The Sox are the toughest ticket in baseball, having sold out every home game since early in the 2003 season and the team currently holds the second longest consecutive-games sellout streak in baseball history.

Numerous factors contribute to the scarcity of available tickets: the allure of Fenway Park itself; the incredible improvements made to the park in recent years; the fact that it has the smallest capacity of any major league ballpark (c. 36,000); the increased fervor generated by the 2004 World Series championship; and the high number of season ticket holders (there is currently a waiting list to buy season tickets). Combine all of that with the legendary zeal New Englanders have for their favorite team and you begin to understand why it is such a hot ticket.

There are many different ways to obtain tickets, whether you buy them directly from the team at face value or from a reseller at a premium price. Of course, buying tickets directly from the team rather than a reseller will almost always be the least expensive and safest way to get tickets.

Buying Directly from the Red Sox

If you want to increase your chances of getting tickets you should start paying attention in December when the team usually puts their first batch of tickets on sale. Over the last few years the team has put tickets for 20 to 25 games on sale about a week or two before Christmas. These are always games in April, May, and September, and most of them are on weeknights (no Yankee games). In other words, school nights with the potential for chilly or rainy weather. This was first done a few years ago as a way to ensure sellouts of April weeknight games which are the hardest games for the team to sell out. Now that sellouts of every game are assured for the foreseeable future, this December on sale date serves the purpose of staggering the on sale dates to give fans more opportunities, and giving fans a chance to buy tickets before the holidays so they can give them as gifts.

33

The tickets for this December on sale date are sold almost entirely sold through redsox.com and the 24-hour touchtone ticketing system (617-482-4769). As with any Red Sox on sale date, the tickets for all affected games usually sell out in a day or less.

The Sox Pax are an excellent deal if you are able to get your hands on one. They consist of tickets to 4 games, with at least one or two being a highly sought after game such as the Yankees or Opening Day. There are a number of different game sets available, and the Sox Pax usually go on sale in December or January. There are a limited number of Sox Pax available, so check redsox.com or call the ticket office (877-733-7699) in early December for more information.

Group ticket sales (20 or more for one game) are a great opportunity if you are able to buy them. They usually go on sale in January before tickets for most games are made available to the general public. Group sales are very limited, and due to high demand, the team has had a policy the past several years of selling the majority of group sales to people or organizations that have purchased group tickets in the past. Call the ticket office (877-733-7699) in December or January for more information.

Tickets for the remainder of the regular season–with the exception of Opening Day and all Yankee games–typically go on sale on a Saturday morning in early February. About 40 to 45 games are available, including all the prime weekend and summer games. Tickets for this on sale date are mainly sold at redsox.com or through the 24-hour touchtone ticketing system (617-482-4769). At the appointed time, legions of fans across New England punch up their Web browsers and sit in the "Virtual Waiting Room" for anywhere from 2 minutes to 20 hours. Many fans never make it to the spine-tingling moment when they actually see tickets offered to them on the Web site. By the end of the day or early the next morning, the Red Sox regular season is basically sold out, and fans who got nothing or didn't get the games they wanted have to look to other ways to obtain tickets.

Yankee games, Green Monster seats, and Right Field Roof Restaurant

Some tickets are so highly sought after that the team decided a few years ago to make them available to the general public only through a lottery system.

By doing this, they hope to increase the chances of average fans getting tickets to the best games and some of the best seats in the park. This includes all tickets to the 9 or 10 Yankee games each year, as well as Green Monster and Right Field Roof Restaurant tickets to all 81 home games. Through a series of staggered lottery drawings in early March, lucky fans who win the lottery are given the opportunity to come back to redsox.com at a specific time and purchase tickets with a special passcode. Fans who win the lottery are usually allowed to buy two or four tickets to one game.

Once the season begins in April each home game has already been classified as a sellout. However, there are still some opportunities for buying tickets from the team if you are patient and persistent. By purchasing a premium membership to Red Sox Nation, the team-sanctioned fan club, you may be given the opportunity to buy tickets to one game. Also, if you have the ability to be spontaneous and decide to go the day before or the day of a game, the Red Sox often release a few hundred tickets shortly before each game. Check redsox.com or call the ticket office (877-733-7699) regularly for availability. You can also call the 24-hour touch tone ticketing system at 617-782-4769, but if you have Internet access, it is usually easier to check at redsox.com.

You can also try going to Fenway the morning of a game as they often have some tickets on hand for walk up sales.

In other words, keep trying. Don't give up just because it appears the season is sold out and you think you may be stuck paying double face value (or more) for tickets from a reseller.

How to Contact the Team about Tickets

24-hour touch tone ticket ordering: 617-482-4769 (617-482-4SOX)
Online ordering: redsox.com
Ticket office at Fenway Park: 877-733-7699 (877-RED-SOX9)
Open Monday through Friday, 10 a.m. to 5 p.m.

If you have any questions about how to obtain tickets from the Red Sox, you can contact them in the following ways:

Mail: Boston Red Sox
4 Yawkey Way
Boston, MA
02215-3496

Phone: 617-267-9440

To order tickets to accommodate fans with disabilities, call 877-733-7699.

Buying Tickets from Resellers

When fans aren't able to buy tickets from the team, or if they can't obtain the type of seats they desire, they often turn to resellers. To see many different tickets offered for sale for all the games, you can go to Ebay, Stubhub.com or any number of different online ticket brokers. To find ticket brokers, just go to Google or Yahoo and search for "Red Sox tickets." Look carefully at the tickets offered at different ticket broker sites. You will usually find that many of them are offering the same exact tickets. This is because in order to increase their available inventory, ticket brokers pool their ticket listings to they can be displayed on many different sites. Usually the prices are the same from site to site, but often they are not.

There is no specific going rate for tickets, but in general you can obtain tickets at Ebay or Stubhub.com for about double the ticket's face value. Prices from ticket brokers tend to start higher than that, and of course, the better the seats and the more desirable the game, the higher the markup.

If you want to go to a Yankee game, the cost of buying from a reseller can be shocking. No matter which type of reseller you look at, you are likely to find prices starting at five times the face value.

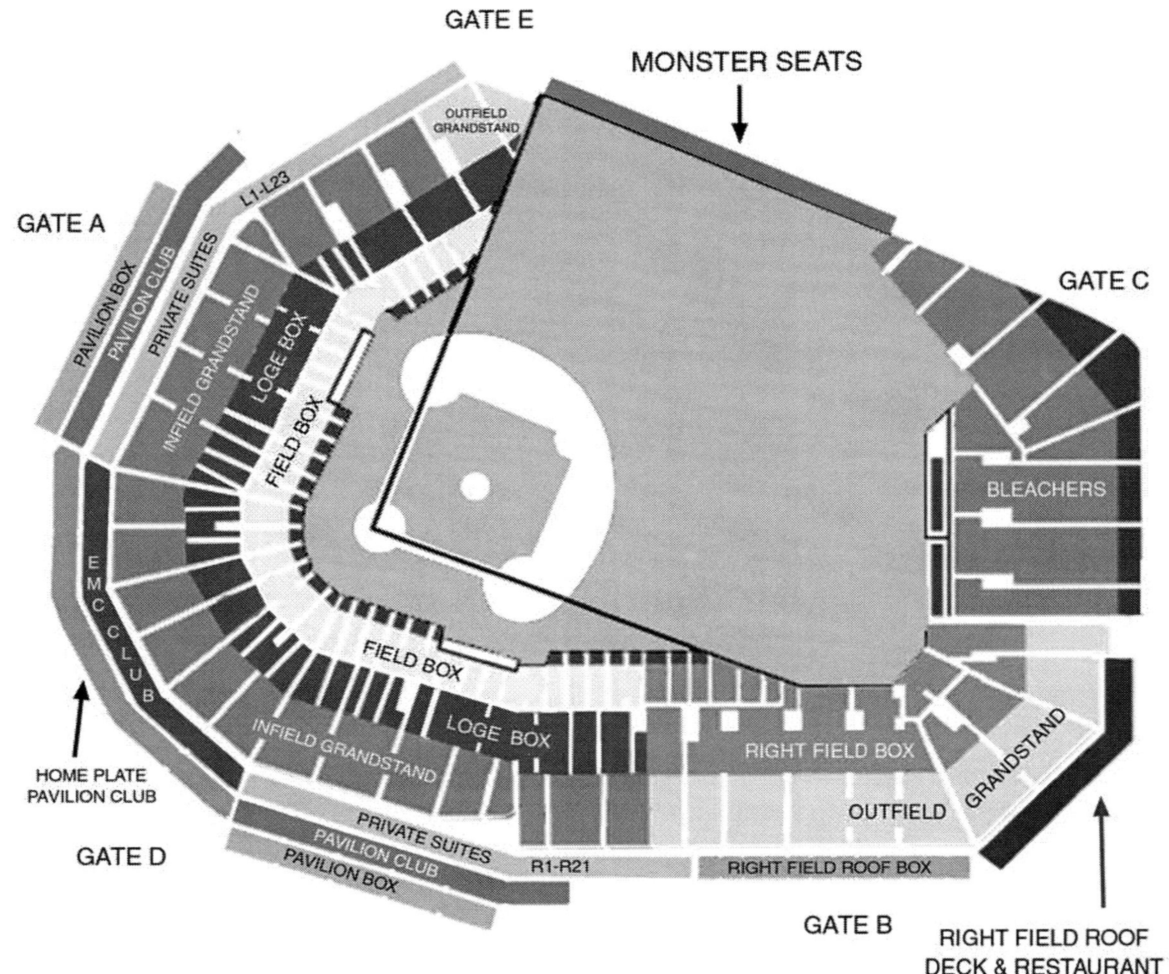

2006 Seating and Pricing

Field Box	$95
Loge Box	$85
Right Field Box	$45
Right Field Roof Box	$45
Infield Grandstand	$45
Outfield Grandstand	$27
Lower Bleachers	$23
Upper Bleachers	$12
Standing Room	$20

Green Monster	
Front Row	$110 - $130
2nd & 3rd Rows	$90 - $110
Standing Room	$25 - $30
Pavilion Level	
EMC Club	$275
Home Plate Pavilion	$195
1st and 3rd Base Pavilion	$150
Pavilion Box	$90
Standing Room	$25
Right Field Roof Restaurant	$90 - $115
Standing Room	$25 - $30

Types of Seating

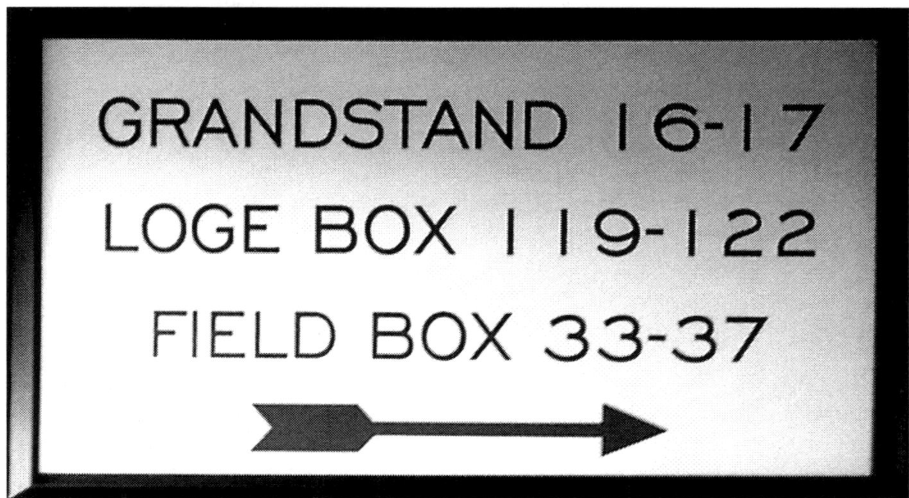

Infield Grandstand

Face value of tickets is $45

Comprised of sections 11-31, the Infield Grandstand sections are located directly behind the Loge Box sections and they run from the middle of the right field line (Section 11) to the middle of the left field line (Section 31), forming a horseshoe around the infield.

Along with the Outfield Grandstand sections, these seats can be affected by pole obstructions. For more information on the location of the poles, see the diagrams in the second half of this book. In general, Infield Grandstand seats are the best seats the average fan can expect to be able to buy from the team. This is because the vast majority of Loge Box and Field Box seats are sold to season ticket holders. There are standing room tickets available ($20) and hundreds of fans stand behind the Infield Grandstand sections during each game.

Outfield Grandstand

Face value of tickets is $27

Comprised of sections 1-10 and 32-33, the Outfield Grandstand sections are located next to the outer edges of the Infield Grandstand sections.

The Outfield Grandstand sections located in right field (1-10) are some of the least sought after seats in the park due to their location and the odd way that many of the sections face center and left fields, rather than the infield. Sections 1 through 3 face the infield, but are extremely far from home plate. Sections 4 through 10 are closer to home plate, but face center and left fields. If you sit in sections 4 through 10 you will spend most of the game looking to your left over the heads of hundreds of fans and it can be a pain in the neck, literally.

The sections in left field (32 and 33) are no alcohol, family sections. Seats in these two sections offer some of the best values in the park. The seats are close to the field and the Green Monster and they face the infield. These seats can be affected by pole obstructions. For more information on the location of the poles, see the diagrams in the second half of this book.

Loge Box

Face value of tickets is $85

The Loge Box sections are situated between the Grandstand and Field Box sections. They run from halfway down the right field line all the way around the infield until just before the Green Monster. Generally speaking, they offer a great view of the park.

The vast majority of these tickets are owned by season ticket holders. The Loge Box sections are in front of the poles, and only a handful of seats have any pole issues whatsoever.

One thing to keep in mind if you have the opportunity to buy Loge Box seats: the first two rows (AA and BB) can be affected by walkway traffic which can make it very difficult to enjoy the game. If possible, check to see if there is a walkway near the seats you are considering buying.

Field Box

Face value of tickets is $95

Field Box sections are located on the field from halfway down the right field line to halfway down the left field line. They are closer to the action than any other seats in the park and they are almost all owned by season ticket holders.

Right Field Box

Face value of tickets is $45

Right Field Box sections are located in front of Grandstand sections 1 through 10. The majority of these seats are very good as they are close to the field and are reasonably priced.

Lower Bleachers

Face value of tickets is $23

Lower Bleacher seats are misnamed because they actually aren't bleachers; the flat metal benches were taken out two decades ago and replaced by actual individual seats. The bleachers are located in center field (sections 34-40) and right field (sections 41-43).

The vast majority of bleacher seats are classified as "Lower Bleachers." The bleachers have plusses and minuses. If you sit there you know you won't ever have to deal with a pole affecting your view. However, you are far from home plate and you are open to the elements, especially the sun and rain. If you get seats in Sections 40-43, you may want to get seats above the fifth row to avoid having to look through a metal screen that separates the bleachers from the bullpens.

Upper Bleachers

Face value of tickets is $12

The Upper Bleacher sections 36-43 are located in the last 5 to 10 rows of each of those sections, usually at least 40 rows up. The team introduced these lower-priced bleacher seats about 5 years ago as a way to offer some of the seats in the park at a very affordable level. The $12 price has held steady for several years.

The Upper Bleacher seats are further from home plate than any other seats in the park, but being so high up, they often are treated to cool breezes on hot days.

Green Monster

Face value of tickets is from $90 to $130

Introduced several years ago to a tremendous amount of fanfare, the Green Monster seats are some of the most expensive, and highly sought after, seats in the park. There are only about 275 Green Monster seats, and given the love Sox fans have for their famous green wall, it is easy to understand why they are so popular. The seats are only sold through the preseason ticket lotteries that usually occur in March. Go to redsox.com in January or February to enter the lottery. There are standing room tickets available ($25-$30), and those are sold to winners of the ticket lottery as well.

EMC Club

Face value of tickets is $275

New for 2006, the EMC Club replaces the .406 Club. Unlike the .406 Club these seats directly behind home plate are open to the elements as the glass windows were removed over the winter. At $275 a ticket it is unlikely that the average fan will ever watch a game from the EMC Club unless someone gives him a ticket.

Home Plate Pavilion Club

Face value of tickets is $195

Located above the EMC Club, these exclusive seats are also sold to season ticket holders. Another new section for 2006, these seats provide a great view of the field, but the cost is prohibitive for the average fan.

First and Third Base Pavilion Club

Face value of tickets is $150

These seats just above the first and third base lines are located in the spot where the seats used to be called first and third base infield roof box seats. New for 2006, they are excellent seats for viewing the game.

Pavilion Box

Face value of tickets is $90

These seats just above the first and third base lines are located above the First and Third Base Pavilion Club seats. New for 2006, they are part of the revamping of the upper level that took place in the winter of 2005-2006. Standing room tickets are available for $25.

Right Field Roof Box

Face value of tickets is $45

Perched above Outfield Grandstand sections 5-9, these open-air seats offer a sparkling view of the entire park at a reasonable price. They are also located next to the Right Field Roof Deck Restaurant.

Right Field Roof Deck Restaurant

Face value of tickets is from $90 to $115

Constructed several years ago on the roof above Outfield Grandstand sections 1 through 4, the Right Field Roof Deck Restaurant has a full menu, but to eat at one of the home plate-shaped tables you must have tickets for them. The opportunity to buy those tickets is obtained through a lottery that is usually held in March. Go to redsox.com in January or February to enter the lottery. Tickets are $90 or $115, and the price of each ticket includes $25 towards your food bill. Standing room tickets for this area are available for $25 - $30, but these are also sold to the winners of the ticket lottery in March.

Getting There and Parking

Most people who don't live in Boston get to Fenway by either driving or taking the "T," which is the greater Boston subway system.

Driving to Fenway

Driving can be a challenge, with the heavy city traffic and the difficulty you may have finding Fenway if you aren't familiar with downtown Boston. If you do drive, there are many different approaches, but if you are coming from the north, west, or south of the city, it is a good idea to take the Mass Pike (I-90) East to Exit 18-Cambridge and then follow these directions:

- Exit at Cambridge tolls and proceeds towards Cambridge
- Turn right onto Storrow Drive East (don't go over the Charles River bridge into Cambridge)
- Continue on Storrow Drive and take the Fenway exit
- After exiting, turn right onto Boylston Street and look for game parking

If you don't mind a 15-minute walk to the park, you can keep it simple by staying on the Mass Pike and getting off at Exit 22-Prudential Center and park in the Prudential Center garage. It is a 1-mile walk from the garage to the park.

If you get lost while driving, try to find your way to Kenmore Square. Once there, turn onto Brookline Avenue and you will be at Fenway after going over the Mass Pike.

Parking

There are lots ringing the park on Brookline Avenue and Boylston Street, with the biggest lot being on Brookline Avenue next to Boston Beer Works. If you park within a 5-minute walk to the park, the fee is usually $25 to $35. Two lots that are very convenient to the park and usually have spaces at least 1 hour before the game are the McDonald's restaurant lot on the corner of Boylston and Jersey streets, and a lot that is steps away from the player's entrance and Gate D on Jersey and Van Ness streets.

Taking the T

If you take the T, you want to get to the Green Line and get off at the Kenmore stop. If you are on the D branch of the Green Line you can also get off at the Fenway stop. At either stop, it is only a few minutes walk to the park.

One common way to avoid driving all the way into Boston is to go to exit 22 on I-95/128 and park at the Riverside MBTA Station. From the north or south you can simply get off at that exit. From the west you can take the Mass Pike to the I-95/128 exit 14, then go south on I-95/128 for 1 mile until you get to exit 22.

There is a 925-space parking lot at the Riverside Station. The fee to park is $3.25 and the subway fare is $3 for adults and $1.50 for kids. If you get on the T at the Fenway station after the game the outbound trip is free. It is a 30-minute ride on the T from the Riverside Station to the park. For more information visit mbta.com or call 617-222-3200.

Taking the Fenway Tour

Touring Fenway makes a great addition to your visit to the park. Tours leave 7 days a week from 9 a.m. to 4 p.m. from the Souvenir Store on Yawkey Way, which is across the street from the main entrance to the park. The cost is $12 for adults and $10 for children and the tours last just about 1 hour.

On game days, the last tour begins 3 hours before the scheduled start time. The last tour of the day on game days is abbreviated, so if you are going to a 2 p.m. Sunday game or 7 p.m. night game it is recommended that you don't go on the last tour so you will be able to experience as much as possible.

In addition to learning a great deal about the park's history from the guides, some of the tour stops include:

- Green Monster seats
- the press box
- the new Pavilion Club
- a walk around the warning track, which gives you the opportunity to take pictures in front of the Green Monster
- the dugout

If you have tickets to a 7 p.m. game and you want to make a full day of your Fenway experience, here is a suggested itinerary:

- take the noon or 1 p.m. tour
- when the tour is over, go Gate D to watch the players come in and give the kids a chance to get autographs (2 to 4 p.m.)
- go to dinner
- back to the park when the gates open at 5 p.m. to watch batting practice and settle in for the game

To contact the Red Sox regarding tours, call 617-226-6666, or email tours@redsox.com. You may want to call ahead to make sure the tour time you have selected has not been cancelled for that day. You can also obtain tour information at redsox.com.

Where to Eat and Drink Before or After the Game

All of the restaurants listed in this section are less than a 10-minute walk to Fenway. They all have menus diverse enough for kids, but the restaurants closest to Fenway (less than a 5-minute walk) do get extremely crowded during the two hours before a game.

TIPS

- Visit the Web site and/or call the restaurant for more detailed information
- If driving, try to make sure you pick a parking lot that is on the same side of the park as where you plan to eat
- If you don't want a long wait for a table and enjoy a less crowded scene, pick a restaurant that is a 5 to 10 minute walk to the park

Boston Beer Works
61 Brookline Ave.
617-536-BEER beerworks.net walking distance to Fenway: 1 minute
Just outside the park near Gate E, this lively and large restaurant and brewpub offers microbrews and a diverse menu to please any taste. If it's not too crowded (you'll often see long lines waiting to get in before a game) the variety and quality of the food makes it a good place for kids.

Cask'n Flagon
62 Brookline Ave.
617-536-4840 casknflagon.com walking distance to Fenway: 1 minute
Located across the street from Fenway near Gate E, this is the oldest and most famous sports bar in the area. Serves a full menu of appetizers, sandwiches, burgers, ribs, and steaks.

Game On!
82 Lansdowne St.
617-351-7001 gameonboston.com walking distance to Fenway: 1 minute
This is a big-time sports bar located inside Fenway Park, just across the street from the Cask'n Flagon. You cannot enter the game through the restaurant. It features 70 high-definition TVs and its menu includes appetizers, salads, burgers, sandwiches, and brick oven pizzas.

Tiki Room
1 Lansdowne St.
617-351-2580 tikiroomboston.com walking distance to Fenway: 1 minute
Fruity, exotic drinks, a faux tropical atmosphere, and interesting platters for groups or families are what you will find at this spot just past center field in the nightclub area of Lansdowne Street.

Jillian's
145 Ipswich St.
617-437-0300 jilliansboston.com walking distance to Fenway: 1 minute
A self-proclaimed "70,000 square foot food entertainment universe," Jillian's is on the second floor of a three-story building that includes a nightclub on the first floor, Tequila Rain, and bowling on the third floor at Lucky Strike. Jillian's boasts numerous pool tables and has a reasonably priced menu (everything under $10) of appetizers, sandwiches, salads, and pizzas. Located next to the Tiki Room.

Canestaro's Restaurant and Pizzeria
16 Peterborough St.
617-266-8997 canestaros.com walking distance to Fenway: 8 minutes
This charming Italian restaurant and pizzeria is tucked away in a quiet residential neighborhood a short walk from Fenway. It serves outstanding Italian food and pizza at reasonable prices and is a great spot for relaxing before or after a game.

El Pelón Taqueria
92 Peterborough St.
617-262-9090 elpelon.com walking distance to Fenway: 7 minutes
Just want a quick bite? Stop by this authentic taqueria for a quick, inexpensive, tasty burrito. Most meals are less than $5. No beer available.

If you don't have time for a sit-down meal, there are plenty of carts on the streets around the park serving up all kinds of hot sandwiches, particularly on Lansdowne Street behind the Green Monster.

Thornton's Fenway Grille
100 Peterborough St.
617-421-0104   walking distance to Fenway: 7 minutes
A lengthy, varied menu and relaxed sidewalk patio make this one of the better pre-game options within walking distance. Known for its casual atmosphere and friendly wait staff this is a great choice for any family or group.

Brown Sugar Cafe
129 Jersey St.
617-266-2928 brownsugarcafe.com walking distance to Fenway: 6 minutes
Considered by many to have the best Thai food in Boston, this charming spot has a diverse menu and a second location at 1033 Commonwealth Ave.

Great Bay
500 Commonwealth Ave.
617-532-5300 greatbayrestaurant.com walking distance to Fenway: 7 minutes
Located in the Hotel Commonwealth in Kenmore Square, this first-class seafood restaurant opened in 2003 and has received rave reviews for its cuisine and ambience. Entrees are about $20 to $25 and reservations are recommended.

Ankara Cafe
472 Commonwealth Ave.
617-437-0404 ankaracafe.com walking distance to Fenway: 8 minutes
This tiny Turkish eatery in Kenmore Square offers authentic Mediterranean food for $5 to $8 a meal, and boasts more than 60 flavors of frozen yogurt. Definitely not fancy, but good, quick, and cheap.

India Quality
484 Commonwealth Ave.
617-267-4499 walking distance to Fenway: 8 minutes
Located in Kenmore Square, one diner called this restaurant a "hidden jewel in downtown Boston." It has received Zagat's Best of Boston award for Indian food and has a large dining room.

Pizzeria Uno
645 Beacon St.
617-262-4911 pizzeriauno.com walking distance to Fenway: 4 minutes
Deep-dish Chicago style pizza, a full Italian menu, and more await at this consistently good chain restaurant.

Eating and Drinking in the Park

While the physical improvements and new seats in the park have garnered the most attention in recent years, the improvements to the quality and variety of food and beverages have probably had a greater impact on the average fan's experience. If you were sitting in Section 32, row 10 in 1999, and you sit there in 2006, your experience of watching the game has not changed much at all. However, your access to high quality food, beverages, and more comfortable areas to consume them has improved immeasurably.

It was only about 5 years ago when the fare inside Fenway was generally limited to hot dogs, sausage, french fries, and pretzels. For beer, you usually had to choose between Bud Light and Coors Light.

Fast forward to 2006 and your choices include Philly Cheesesteaks, El Tiante Cuban sandwiches, barbecued chicken, humongous hot dogs at RemDawg's, clam chowder, and more. Beer options include Sam Adams in several areas of the park, as well as Guinness, Harp, and Smithwick's, which are only available near section 19. Frozen margaritas and daiquiris are available near section 26.

Since late in the 2003 season the portion of Yawkey Way that runs from Gate A to Gate D has essentially become part of the ballpark for two hours prior to and during the entire game. The team received permission from the city of Boston to close that portion of the street off so that it can be used only by fans with tickets to the game. This means that more concessions are available to fans throughout the game, including El Tiante's and RemDawg's. It also means that fans have access to the huge souvenir store on Yawkey Way during the entire game.

The areas inside the park to buy and eat your food have also been improved

SOX

dramatically. A couple of years ago the team cleared out some space in right field and behind the bleachers and created a huge open-air concourse for concessions, complete with picnic tables and TV monitors to watch the game. Similarly, the left field concession area has been expanded and includes several huge plasma TVs to watch the game while you wait for your food.

There are also new and improved concession areas on the Green Monster and in the Pavilion sections, but you must be ticketed for those sections to get in.

The Right Field Roof Deck Restaurant has a full menu, but to eat at one of the home plate-shaped tables you must have tickets for them. The opportunity to buy those tickets is obtained through a lottery that is usually held in March. Tickets for 2006 are $90 or $115, and the price of each ticket includes $25 towards your food bill.

What all these improvements mean is that you no longer have to eat before you come into the game if you want a variety of tasty things to eat. If you want to enjoy the park when it is not crowded and catch batting practice, the gates open 2 hours prior to the scheduled start time.

WHO'S
YOUR
PAPI?

JETER
DRINKS
WINE
COOLERS

LOOKS LIKE JESUS
THROWS LIKE MARY
ACTS LIKE JUDAS
JOHNNY BE GONE!

LOVE ME,
ORTIZ ME?

WORST CHOKE IN
SPORTS HISTORY

The Rivalry with the Yankees

If you want to understand the intensity of the rivalry between the Red Sox and Yankees, all you need to do is consider the receptions given to departed Sox stars Pedro Martinez and Johnny Damon upon their returns to Fenway Park. Both players, having left the Red Sox after being offered more money as free agents from New York teams, came back in highly anticipated debuts as opposing players in the first half of the 2006 season. Pedro, returning as a pitcher for the New York Mets, was treated like the baseball god of Beantown he was for seven years. He was cheered loudly and lovingly whenever he appeared on the field, and he basked in the glow of the fans' adulation. Damon, who actually had much more to do with the Red Sox winning the World Series in 2004 than Pedro, was booed unmercifully when he came back clean shaven and wearing the hated drab, gray uniform of the Evil Empire. It was then that Johnny may have realized what he sacrificed when he went for the money: if he stayed in Boston he would have been treated like a king forever as the man who almost single-handedly won Game 7 of the 2004 ALCS against the Yankees; but in New York, if he doesn't win the World Series every year, he is just another overpaid bum.

The baseball life of a Red Sox fan for most of the twentieth century was defined by feeling inferior to the Yankees. And with good reason: from 1923 through 2000 the Yankees won 26 World Series titles while the Red Sox won zero. (Curse of the Bambino, Bucky Dent, Bill Buckner, etc. You know the stories). But then in 2001 things began to gradually change to the delight of Sox fans everywhere. The Yankees, while seemingly having their fifth World Series title in six years all sewn up, lost in the ninth inning of Game 7 to the Arizona Diamondbacks. The loss was stunning and excruciating (for Yankee fans). With the best relief pitcher in the history of baseball on the mound, the Yankees coughed up the lead and lost on a walkoff bloop single to shortstop. The loss was, well, almost Soxian.

In 2003 the Red Sox and Yankees met in the ALCS for the second time. There was a brawl in Game 3 and Pedro tossed 72-year-old Yankees bench coach Don Zimmer to the ground. Game 7 was a bona fide horror show for Sox fans: manager Grady Little left Pedro in too long as he coughed up a 4-0 lead, and Aaron Boone hit a walkoff home run off Tim Wakefield in extra innings. People all over New England wanted to go to bed and not get up for about six months. But Sox fans were buoyed when the Yankees again lost the World Series in improbable fashion, blowing a 2 games to 1 series lead and losing the last 3 games of the series to the Florida Marlins, including getting shut out at Yankee Stadium in series-ending Game 6.

2004 was, of course, the greatest year in Sox history. The heroics of David Ortiz, Curt Schilling, Johnny Damon, and so many others are well chronicled. They vanquished their unvanquishable foe in the Yankees and did it in a way that no one will ever forget. Sox fans could finally shed their feelings of inferiority. And with good reason: as Jason Varitek said before the World Series victory parade in Boston, Sox fans can now walk into Yankee Stadium with their heads held high.

Following the 2004 season Yankee fans wallowed in utter humiliation. They didn't have much to say about the Sox and their fans. The unthinkable, unimaginable, and impossible had happened. As one New York tabloid headline read the day after the Yankees lost the ALCS to the Red Sox, *Hell Freezes Over*. It was only after the Chicago White Sox won the 2005 World Series that Yankee fans started to crawl out of their holes. T-shirts with references to the Yankees overall historical dominance of the Red Sox began to appear. These include: *Got Rings?*, *Yankee Universe*, and *Do the Math*. Here's some math: What are the odds that a team with a 3-0 series lead that is winning in the ninth inning of Game 4 with the greatest relief pitcher in the history of baseball on the mound could find a way to blow that game and the next three? About a bazillion to one? Or try this math: $200 million player payroll = 0 championships.

What does all this mean to fans who want to go see the Yankees play the Sox at Fenway? The games are much more intense, the energy in the park is much higher than usual, and tickets are much harder to come by. Your best shot at getting tickets for a reasonable cost is to either win the ticket purchasing opportunity lottery or find a friend or business associate who can get you tickets. Other than that, you can expect to pay, pay, pay for the privilege of watching the greatest rivalry in sports.

Understanding the Seating Diagrams

ROW												
10	1	2	3	4	5	6	7	8	9	10	11	12
9	1	2	3	4	5	6	7	8	9	10	11	12
8	1	2	3	4	5	6	7	8	9	10	11	12
7	1	2	3	4	5	6	7	8	9	10	11	12
6	1	2	3	4	5	6	7	8	9	10	11	12
5	1	2	3	4	5	6	7	8	9	10	11	12
4	1	2	3	4	5	6	7	8	9	10	11	12
3	1	2	3	4	5	6	7	8	9	10	11	12
2	1	2	3	4	5	6	7	8	9	10	11	12
1	1	2	3	4	5	6	7	8	9	10	11	12

Detail of Section 12 Seating Diagram
Bold numbers running vertically are row numbers
Numbers in boxes running horizontally are seat numbers

The seating diagrams in this book are intended to help you identify the seats in Grandstand sections that have **a pole impeding your view of home plate, the pitcher's mound, or both.**

As you can see in this detail from Section 12, the shaded areas cover seats that have a pole between them and either home plate or the pitcher's mound. In this case, the shaded area on the right has a home plate obstruction, and the shaded area on the left has a pitcher's mound obstruction.

So, if you sit in Section 12, Row 7, Seat 7 you will have difficulty seeing home plate without having to move forward, backward, or side to side. Similarly, if you sit in Row 4, Seat 6 you will have difficulty seeing the pitcher's mound.

Many seat numbers are partially shaded. This means that the pole issues affecting that seat are not as intrusive as seats that are completely shaded. If you're not sure if a seat will have any pole issues by looking at the diagrams, it would be a good idea to pick seats that are at least 2 completely non-shaded seats away from the obstructed area.

Generally, the further back you are in a section, the less of a problem the pole will be for your view. The closer you are to a pole, the bigger it looks.

Section 1

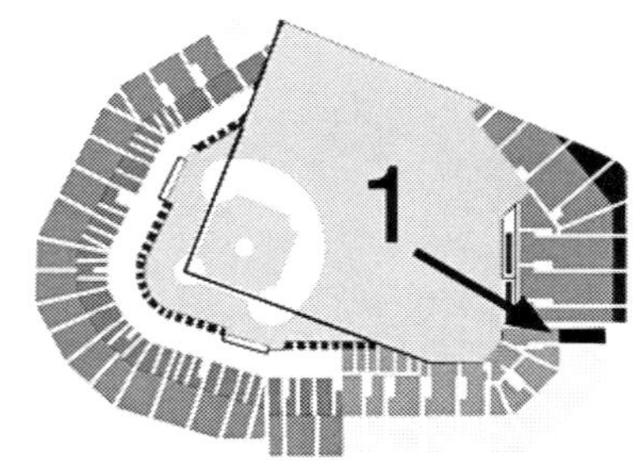

Outfield Grandstand
Face Value of tickets is $27

Section 1 is in right field behind Right Field Box 87.

Section 1 borders the bleacher seats, and the main difference between sitting in Section 1 or rows 15 – 30 of Bleacher Section 43 is that Section 1 is covered by a roof in case it rains. With only 8 seats in each row, it does make the seats feel less congested than most other sections and you have easier access to the seats. Also, unlike many of the other Outfield Grandstand sections, these seats face home plate, and not left field.

There is a pole near row 1, seat 1 that affects that seat and one or two others in each row running diagonally up to row 17, seat 5.

The view from the center of Section 1

Section I

ROW
18
17
16
15
14
13
12
11
10
9
8
7
6
5
4
3
2
1
ROW
home plate

= View of home plate or pitcher's mound is obstructed

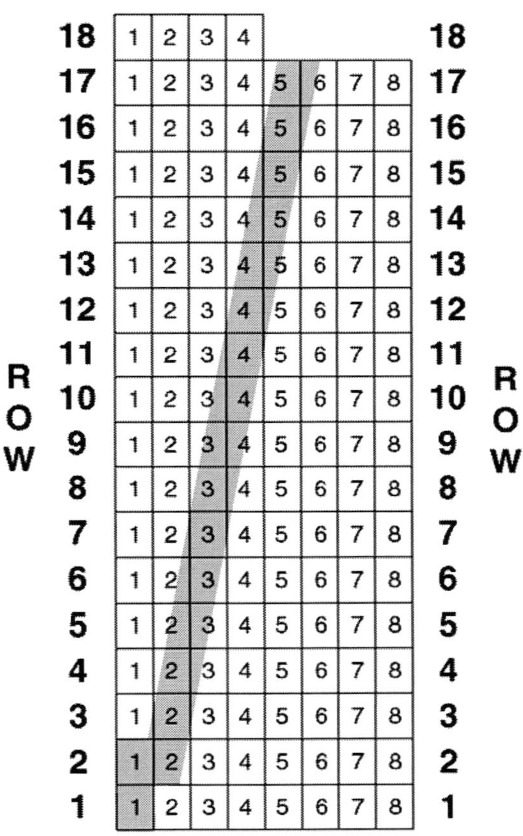

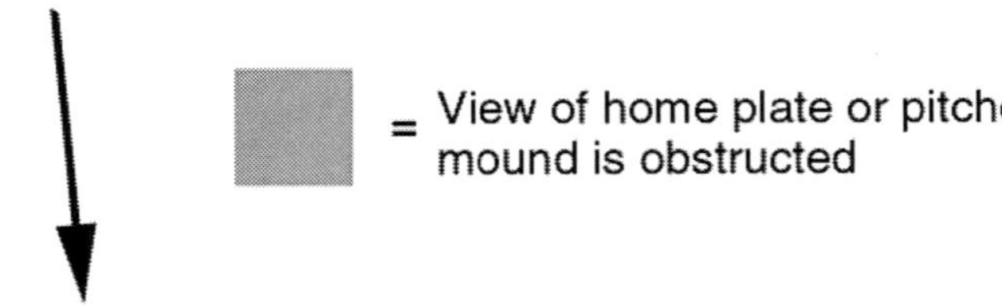

Section 2

Outfield Grandstand
Face Value of tickets is $27

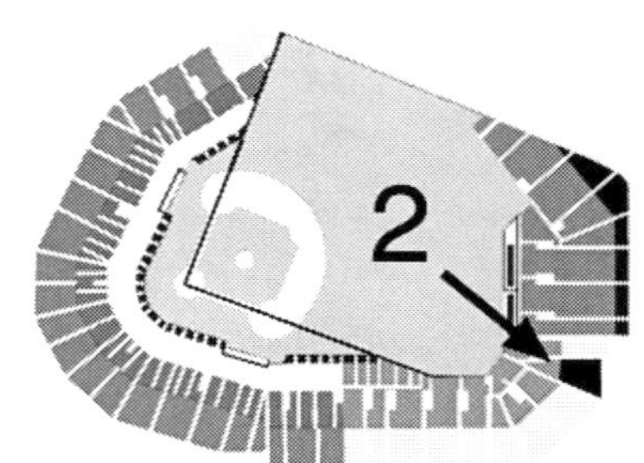

Section 2 is in right field behind Right Field Box 88.

Section 2 is a large section in right field that is far from home plate. Unlike many of the other Outfield Grandstand sections, these seats face home plate, and not left field.

If you are facing the field, pole issues are limited to some seats on the left side of the section. Any seat numbered 1 through 18 is free from poles.

The view from the center of Section 2

Section 2

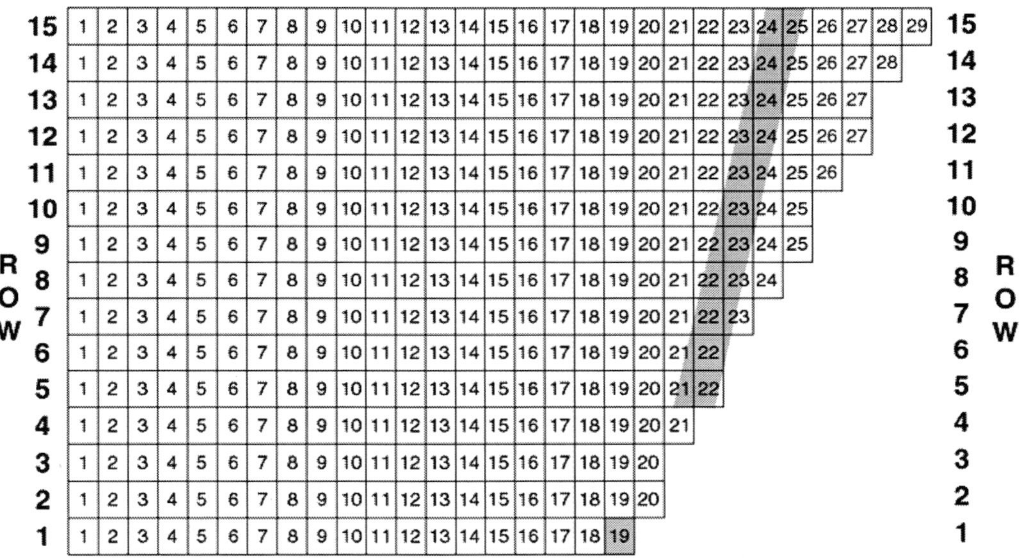

ROW																														ROW
15	1	2	3	4	5	6	7	8	9	10	11	12	13	14	15	16	17	18	19	20	21	22	23	24	25	26	27	28	29	15
14	1	2	3	4	5	6	7	8	9	10	11	12	13	14	15	16	17	18	19	20	21	22	23	24	25	26	27	28		14
13	1	2	3	4	5	6	7	8	9	10	11	12	13	14	15	16	17	18	19	20	21	22	23	24	25	26	27			13
12	1	2	3	4	5	6	7	8	9	10	11	12	13	14	15	16	17	18	19	20	21	22	23	24	25	26	27			12
11	1	2	3	4	5	6	7	8	9	10	11	12	13	14	15	16	17	18	19	20	21	22	23	24	25	26				11
10	1	2	3	4	5	6	7	8	9	10	11	12	13	14	15	16	17	18	19	20	21	22	23	24	25					10
9	1	2	3	4	5	6	7	8	9	10	11	12	13	14	15	16	17	18	19	20	21	22	23	24	25					9
8	1	2	3	4	5	6	7	8	9	10	11	12	13	14	15	16	17	18	19	20	21	22	23	24						8
7	1	2	3	4	5	6	7	8	9	10	11	12	13	14	15	16	17	18	19	20	21	22	23							7
6	1	2	3	4	5	6	7	8	9	10	11	12	13	14	15	16	17	18	19	20	21	22								6
5	1	2	3	4	5	6	7	8	9	10	11	12	13	14	15	16	17	18	19	20	21	22								5
4	1	2	3	4	5	6	7	8	9	10	11	12	13	14	15	16	17	18	19	20	21									4
3	1	2	3	4	5	6	7	8	9	10	11	12	13	14	15	16	17	18	19	20										3
2	1	2	3	4	5	6	7	8	9	10	11	12	13	14	15	16	17	18	19	20										2
1	1	2	3	4	5	6	7	8	9	10	11	12	13	14	15	16	17	18	19											1

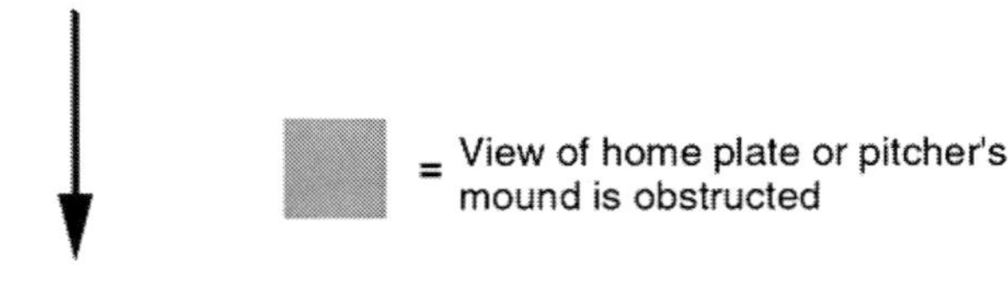

Section 3

Outfield Grandstand
Face Value of tickets is $27

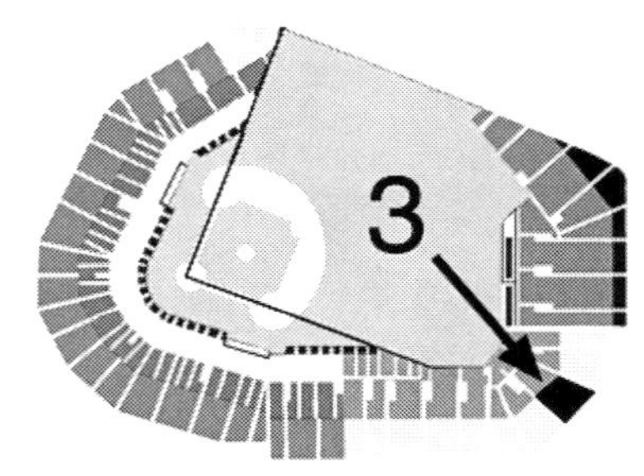

Section 3 is in right field behind Right Field Box 89.

Section 3 is a large section directly down the right field line that is far from home plate. Unlike many of the other Outfield Grandstand sections, these seats face the infield, and not left field.

If you are facing the field, pole issues are limited to some seats on the left side of the section. Beginning in row 4, seat 25, the obstruction affects some seats up to row 15, seat 25. All the seats in rows 1 through 3 are safe from poles, as well as any seats numbered 1 through 22 in the entire section.

The view from the center of Section 3

Section 3

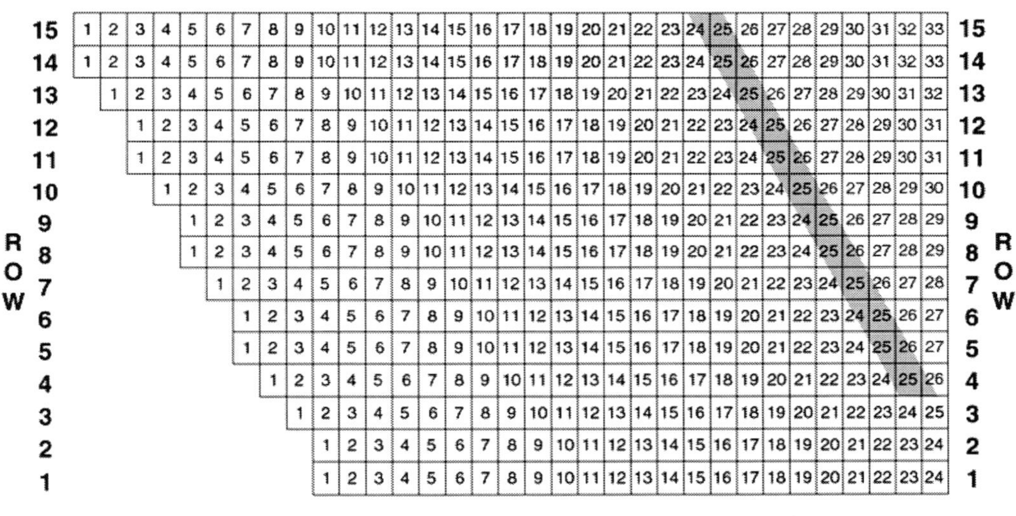

= View of home plate or pitcher's mound is obstructed

home plate

Section 4

Outfield Grandstand
Face Value of tickets is $27

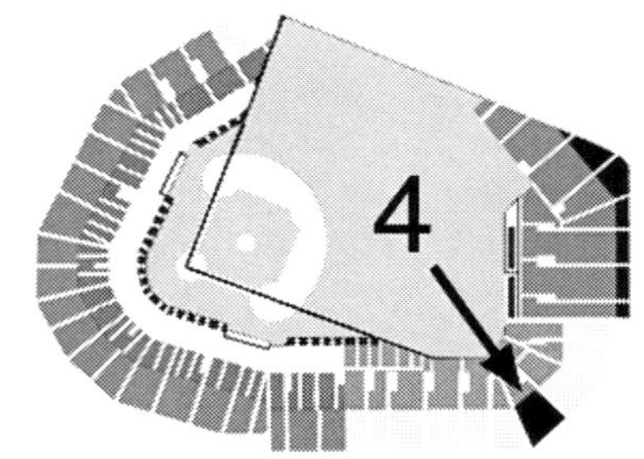

Section 4 is in right field behind Right Field Box 90.

Tucked away in the right field corner, seats in this section are very far from home plate and they face the left field foul pole, rather than the infield, which causes you to have to look to the left to see the action. Although they are fairly priced at $27, these are some of the worst seats in Fenway.

There is a pole that affects seats 26 and 27 in the second row, and the obstruction runs diagonally up through the section to seat 19 in row 17.

The view from the center of Section 4

Section 4

ROW																																						ROW
17	1	2	3	4	5	6	7	8	9	10	11	12	13	14	15	16	17	18	19	20	21	22	23	24	25	26	27	28	29	30	31	32	33	34	35	36	37	17
16	1	2	3	4	5	6	7	8	9	10	11	12	13	14	15	16	17	18	19	20	21	22	23	24	25	26	27	28	29	30	31	32	33	34	35	36		16
15	1	2	3	4	5	6	7	8	9	10	11	12	13	14	15	16	17	18	19	20	21	22	23	24	25	26	27	28	29	30	31	32	33	34	35	36		15
14	1	2	3	4	5	6	7	8	9	10	11	12	13	14	15	16	17	18	19	20	21	22	23	24	25	26	27	28	29	30	31	32	33	34	35			14
13	1	2	3	4	5	6	7	8	9	10	11	12	13	14	15	16	17	18	19	20	21	22	23	24	25	26	27	28	29	30	31	32	33	34				13
12	1	2	3	4	5	6	7	8	9	10	11	12	13	14	15	16	17	18	19	20	21	22	23	24	25	26	27	28	29	30	31	32	33	34				12
11	1	2	3	4	5	6	7	8	9	10	11	12	13	14	15	16	17	18	19	20	21	22	23	24	25	26	27	28	29	30	31	32	33					11
10	1	2	3	4	5	6	7	8	9	10	11	12	13	14	15	16	17	18	19	20	21	22	23	24	25	26	27	28	29	30	31	32						10
9	1	2	3	4	5	6	7	8	9	10	11	12	13	14	15	16	17	18	19	20	21	22	23	24	25	26	27	28	29	30	31	32						9
8	1	2	3	4	5	6	7	8	9	10	11	12	13	14	15	16	17	18	19	20	21	22	23	24	25	26	27	28	29	30	31							8
7	1	2	3	4	5	6	7	8	9	10	11	12	13	14	15	16	17	18	19	20	21	22	23	24	25	26	27	28	29	30								7
6	1	2	3	4	5	6	7	8	9	10	11	12	13	14	15	16	17	18	19	20	21	22	23	24	25	26	27	28	29	30								6
5	1	2	3	4	5	6	7	8	9	10	11	12	13	14	15	16	17	18	19	20	21	22	23	24	25	26	27	28	29									5
4	1	2	3	4	5	6	7	8	9	10	11	12	13	14	15	16	17	18	19	20	21	22	23	24	25	26	27	28										4
3	1	2	3	4	5	6	7	8	9	10	11	12	13	14	15	16	17	18	19	20	21	22	23	24	25	26	27	28										3
2	1	2	3	4	5	6	7	8	9	10	11	12	13	14	15	16	17	18	19	20	21	22	23	24	25	26	27											2
1	1	2	3	4	5	6	7	8	9	10	11	12	13	14	15	16	17	18	19	20	21	22	23	24	25	26												1

= View of home plate or pitcher's mound is obstructed

home plate

Section 5

Outfield Grandstand
Face Value of tickets is $27

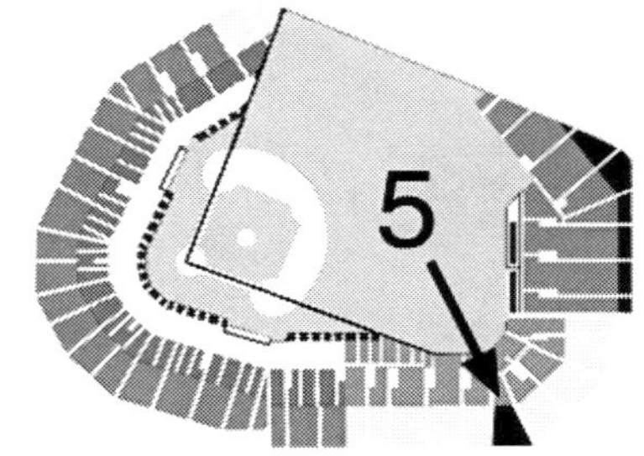

Section 5 is in right field behind Right Field Box 91.

Tucked away in the right field corner, seats in this section are very far from home plate and they face the Green Monster, rather than the infield, which causes you to have to look to the left to see the action. Although they are fairly priced at $27, these are some of the worst seats in Fenway.

There is a pole obstruction that runs diagonally across the section from the last few seats in row 3 to the first few seats in row 9. All seats in rows 1, 2, and 10-17 are free from pole issues.

The view from the center of Section 5

Section 5

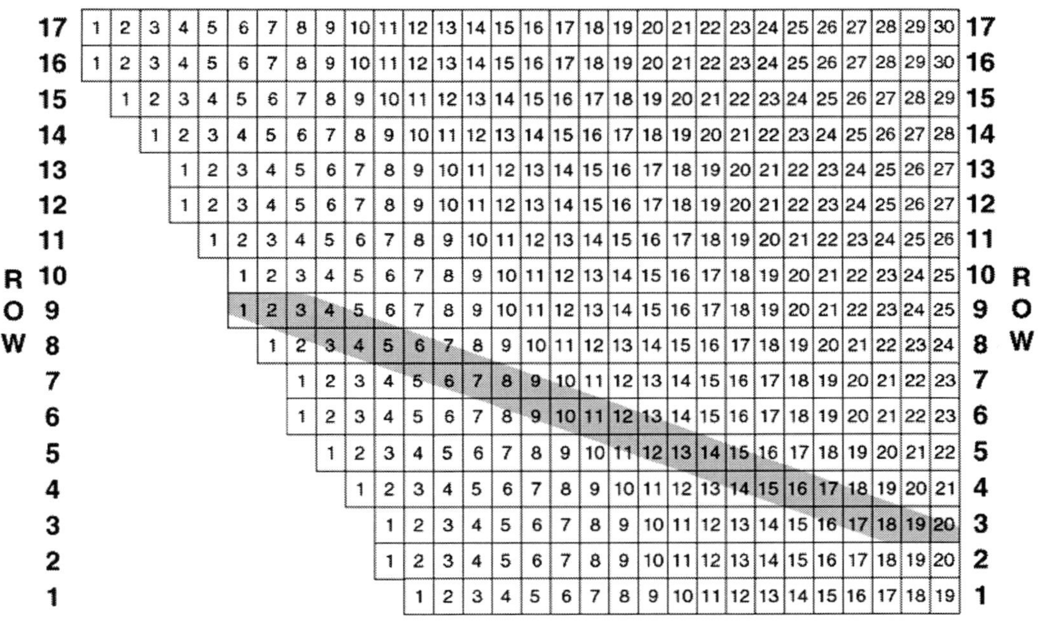

= View of home plate or pitcher's mound is obstructed

home plate

Section 6

Outfield Grandstand
Face Value of tickets is $27

Section 6 is in right field behind Right Field Box 92.

Tucked away in the right field corner, seats in this section are far from home plate and they face center field, rather than the infield, which causes you to have to look to the left to see the action. Compared to most other sections in the park, these are not very good seats.

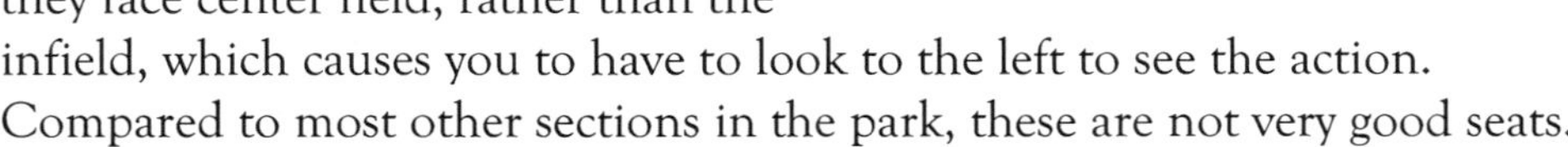

There is a pole obstruction that runs from the last few seats in rows 4 and 5 diagonally across the section to the first seat in row 12. All seats in rows 1-3 and 13-17 are free from pole issues.

The view from the center of Section 6

Section 6

17	1	2	3	4	5	6	7	8	9	10	11	12	13	14	15	16	17	18	19	20	21	17
16	1	2	3	4	5	6	7	8	9	10	11	12	13	14	15	16	17	18	19	20	21	16
15	1	2	3	4	5	6	7	8	9	10	11	12	13	14	15	16	17	18	19	20	21	15
14	1	2	3	4	5	6	7	8	9	10	11	12	13	14	15	16	17	18	19	20	21	14
13	1	2	3	4	5	6	7	8	9	10	11	12	13	14	15	16	17	18	19	20	21	13
12	1	2	3	4	5	6	7	8	9	10	11	12	13	14	15	16	17	18	19	20	21	12
11	1	2	3	4	5	6	7	8	9	10	11	12	13	14	15	16	17	18	19	20	21	11
R 10	1	2	3	4	5	6	7	8	9	10	11	12	13	14	15	16	17	18	19	20	21	10 R
O 9	1	2	3	4	5	6	7	8	9	10	11	12	13	14	15	16	17	18	19	20	21	9 O
W 8	1	2	3	4	5	6	7	8	9	10	11	12	13	14	15	16	17	18	19	20	21	8 W
7	1	2	3	4	5	6	7	8	9	10	11	12	13	14	15	16	17	18	19	20	21	7
6	1	2	3	4	5	6	7	8	9	10	11	12	13	14	15	16	17	18	19	20	21	6
5	1	2	3	4	5	6	7	8	9	10	11	12	13	14	15	16	17	18	19	20	21	5
4	1	2	3	4	5	6	7	8	9	10	11	12	13	14	15	16	17	18	19	20	21	4
3	1	2	3	4	5	6	7	8	9	10	11	12	13	14	15	16	17	18	19	20	21	3
2	1	2	3	4	5	6	7	8	9	10	11	12	13	14	15	16	17	18	19	20	21	2
1	1	2	3	4	5	6	7	8	9	10	11	12	13	14	15	16	17	18	19	20	21	1

= View of home plate or pitcher's mound is obstructed

home plate

Section 7

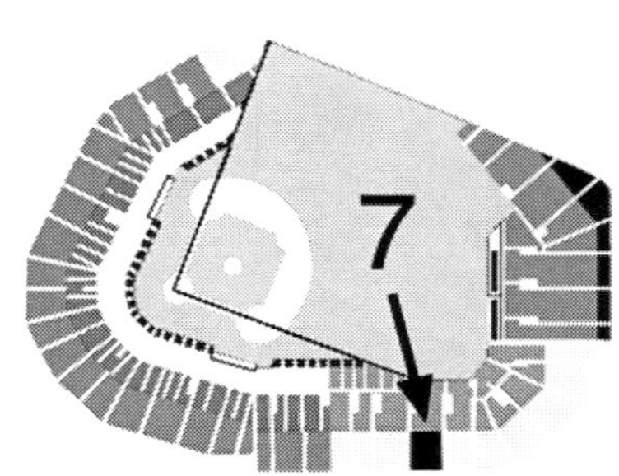

Outfield Grandstand
Face Value of tickets is $27

Section 7 is in right field behind Right Field Box 93.

Located down the right field line past the foul pole, seats in this section are far from home plate and they face left field, rather than the infield, which causes you to have to look to the left to see the action. Compared to most other sections in the park, these are not very good seats.

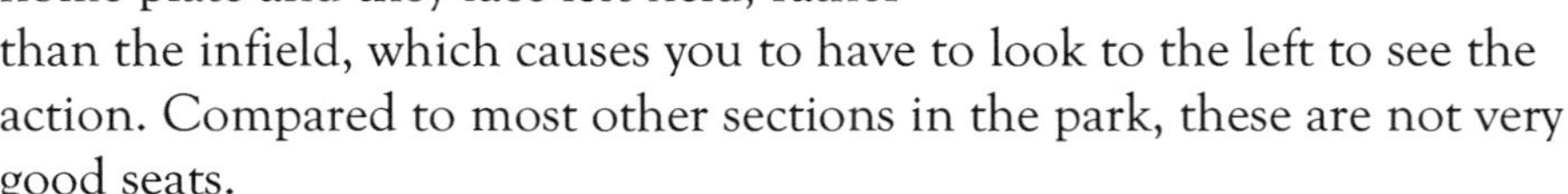

There are two pole obstructions in this section, one that affects the first few rows in the lower-numbered seats, and one that runs diagonally across the middle rows.

The view from the center of Section 7

Section 7

ROW																											ROW
17	1	2	3	4	5	6	7	8	9	10	11	12	13	14	15	16	17	18	19	20	21	22	23	24	25	26	17
16	1	2	3	4	5	6	7	8	9	10	11	12	13	14	15	16	17	18	19	20	21	22	23	24	25	26	16
15	1	2	3	4	5	6	7	8	9	10	11	12	13	14	15	16	17	18	19	20	21	22	23	24	25	26	15
14	1	2	3	4	5	6	7	8	9	10	11	12	13	14	15	16	17	18	19	20	21	22	23	24	25	26	14
13	1	2	3	4	5	6	7	8	9	10	11	12	13	14	15	16	17	18	19	20	21	22	23	24	25	26	13
12	1	2	3	4	5	6	7	8	9	10	11	12	13	14	15	16	17	18	19	20	21	22	23	24	25	26	12
11	1	2	3	4	5	6	7	8	9	10	11	12	13	14	15	16	17	18	19	20	21	22	23	24	25	26	11
10	1	2	3	4	5	6	7	8	9	10	11	12	13	14	15	16	17	18	19	20	21	22	23	24	25	26	10
9	1	2	3	4	5	6	7	8	9	10	11	12	13	14	15	16	17	18	19	20	21	22	23	24	25	26	9
8	1	2	3	4	5	6	7	8	9	10	11	12	13	14	15	16	17	18	19	20	21	22	23	24	25	26	8
7	1	2	3	4	5	6	7	8	9	10	11	12	13	14	15	16	17	18	19	20	21	22	23	24	25	26	7
6	1	2	3	4	5	6	7	8	9	10	11	12	13	14	15	16	17	18	19	20	21	22	23	24	25	26	6
5	1	2	3	4	5	6	7	8	9	10	11	12	13	14	15	16	17	18	19	20	21	22	23	24	25	26	5
4	1	2	3	4	5	6	7	8	9	10	11	12	13	14	15	16	17	18	19	20	21	22	23	24	25	26	4
3	1	2	3	4	5	6	7	8	9	10	11	12	13	14	15	16	17	18	19	20	21	22	23	24	25	26	3
2	1	2	3	4	5	6	7	8	9	10	11	12	13	14	15	16	17	18	19	20	21	22	23	24	25	26	2
1	1	2	3	4	5	6	7	8	9	10	11	12	13	14	15	16	17	18	19	20	21	22	23	24	25	26	1

= View of home plate or pitcher's mound is obstructed

home plate

Section 8

Outfield Grandstand
Face Value of tickets is $27

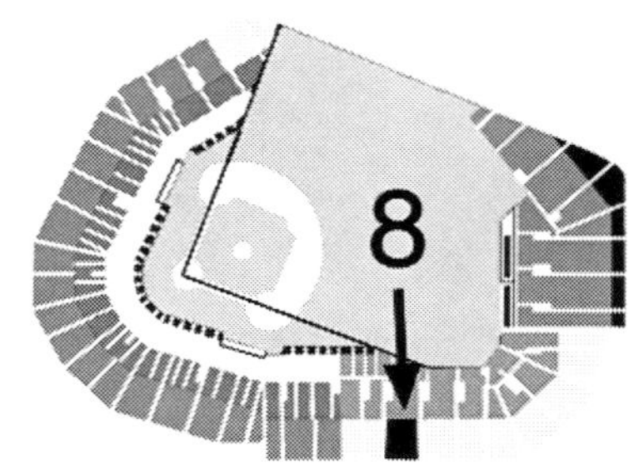

Section 8 is in right field behind Right Field Box 94.

Located down the right field line near the foul pole, seats in this section face left field, rather than the infield, which causes you to have to look to the left to see the action.

There are two pole obstructions in this section, one that affects the first few rows in the lower-numbered seats, and one that runs diagonally across rows 7 through 17.

The view from the center of Section 8

Section 8

ROW																											ROW
17	1	2	3	4	5	6	7	8	9	10	11	12	13	14	15	16	17	18	19	20	21	22	23	24	25	26	17
16	1	2	3	4	5	6	7	8	9	10	11	12	13	14	15	16	17	18	19	20	21	22	23	24	25	26	16
15	1	2	3	4	5	6	7	8	9	10	11	12	13	14	15	16	17	18	19	20	21	22	23	24	25	26	15
14	1	2	3	4	5	6	7	8	9	10	11	12	13	14	15	16	17	18	19	20	21	22	23	24	25	26	14
13	1	2	3	4	5	6	7	8	9	10	11	12	13	14	15	16	17	18	19	20	21	22	23	24	25	26	13
12	1	2	3	4	5	6	7	8	9	10	11	12	13	14	15	16	17	18	19	20	21	22	23	24	25	26	12
11	1	2	3	4	5	6	7	8	9	10	11	12	13	14	15	16	17	18	19	20	21	22	23	24	25	26	11
10	1	2	3	4	5	6	7	8	9	10	11	12	13	14	15	16	17	18	19	20	21	22	23	24	25	26	10
9	1	2	3	4	5	6	7	8	9	10	11	12	13	14	15	16	17	18	19	20	21	22	23	24	25	26	9
8	1	2	3	4	5	6	7	8	9	10	11	12	13	14	15	16	17	18	19	20	21	22	23	24	25	26	8
7	1	2	3	4	5	6	7	8	9	10	11	12	13	14	15	16	17	18	19	20	21	22	23	24	25	26	7
6	1	2	3	4	5	6	7	8	9	10	11	12	13	14	15	16	17	18	19	20	21	22	23	24	25	26	6
5	1	2	3	4	5	6	7	8	9	10	11	12	13	14	15	16	17	18	19	20	21	22	23	24	25	26	5
4	1	2	3	4	5	6	7	8	9	10	11	12	13	14	15	16	17	18	19	20	21	22	23	24	25	26	4
3	1	2	3	4	5	6	7	8	9	10	11	12	13	14	15	16	17	18	19	20	21	22	23	24	25	26	3
2	1	2	3	4	5	6	7	8	9	10	11	12	13	14	15	16	17	18	19	20	21	22	23	24	25	26	2
1	1	2	3	4	5	6	7	8	9	10	11	12	13	14	15	16	17	18	19	20	21	22	23	24	25	26	1

 = View of home plate or pitcher's mound is obstructed

home plate

Section 9

Outfield Grandstand
Face Value of tickets is $27

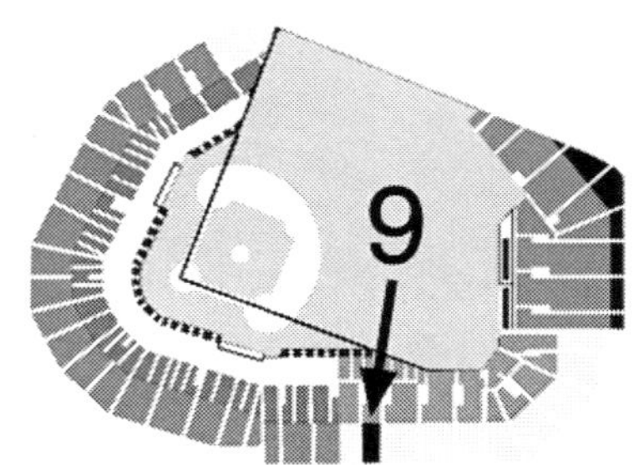

Section 9 is in right field behind Right Field Box 95.

Located down the right field line, seats in this section face left field, rather than the infield, which causes you to have to look to the left to see the action.

There are two pole obstructions in this section, one that affects some seats in rows 1 through 7, and another that affects some seats in rows 14 through 17. All seats in rows 8 through 13 are free from pole issues.

The view from the center of Section 9

Section 9

ROW																	ROW
17	1	2	3	4	5	6	7	8	9	10	11	12	13	14	15	16	17
16	1	2	3	4	5	6	7	8	9	10	11	12	13	14	15	16	16
15	1	2	3	4	5	6	7	8	9	10	11	12	13	14	15	16	15
14	1	2	3	4	5	6	7	8	9	10	11	12	13	14	15	16	14
13	1	2	3	4	5	6	7	8	9	10	11	12	13	14	15	16	13
12	1	2	3	4	5	6	7	8	9	10	11	12	13	14	15	16	12
11	1	2	3	4	5	6	7	8	9	10	11	12	13	14	15	16	11
10	1	2	3	4	5	6	7	8	9	10	11	12	13	14	15	16	10
9	1	2	3	4	5	6	7	8	9	10	11	12	13	14	15	16	9
8	1	2	3	4	5	6	7	8	9	10	11	12	13	14	15	16	8
7	1	2	3	4	5	6	7	8	9	10	11	12	13	14	15	16	7
6	1	2	3	4	5	6	7	8	9	10	11	12	13	14	15	16	6
5	1	2	3	4	5	6	7	8	9	10	11	12	13	14	15	16	5
4	1	2	3	4	5	6	7	8	9	10	11	12	13	14	15	16	4
3	1	2	3	4	5	6	7	8	9	10	11	12	13	14	15	16	3
2	1	2	3	4	5	6	7	8	9	10	11	12	13	14	15	16	2
1	1	2	3	4	5	6	7	8	9	10	11	12	13	14	15	16	1

 = View of home plate or pitcher's mound is obstructed

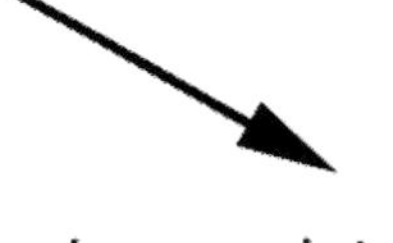

home plate

Section 10

Outfield Grandstand
Face Value of tickets is $27

Section 10 is in right field behind Right Field Box 97.

Located down the right field line, this section is closer to the infield than any other leftfield grandstand section. The seats in neighboring Section 11 have a face value of $45.

There is one obstruction in this section, beginning with the last seat in row 5 moving diagonally to the first seat in row 11. All seats in rows 1-4 and 12-17 are free from poles.

The view from the center of Section 10

Section 10

ROW														ROW
17	1	2	3	4	5	6	7	8	9	10	11	12	13	17
16	1	2	3	4	5	6	7	8	9	10	11	12	13	16
15	1	2	3	4	5	6	7	8	9	10	11	12	13	15
14	1	2	3	4	5	6	7	8	9	10	11	12	13	14
13	1	2	3	4	5	6	7	8	9	10	11	12	13	13
12	1	2	3	4	5	6	7	8	9	10	11	12	13	12
11	1	2	3	4	5	6	7	8	9	10	11	12	13	11
10	1	2	3	4	5	6	7	8	9	10	11	12	13	10
9	1	2	3	4	5	6	7	8	9	10	11	12	13	9
8	1	2	3	4	5	6	7	8	9	10	11	12	13	8
7	1	2	3	4	5	6	7	8	9	10	11	12	13	7
6	1	2	3	4	5	6	7	8	9	10	11	12	13	6
5	1	2	3	4	5	6	7	8	9	10	11	12	13	5
4	1	2	3	4	5	6	7	8	9	10	11	12	13	4
3	1	2	3	4	5	6	7	8	9	10	11	12	13	3
2	1	2	3	4	5	6	7	8	9	10	11	12	13	2
1	1	2	3	4	5	6	7	8	9	10	11	12	13	1

= View of home plate or pitcher's mound is obstructed

home plate

Section 11

Infield Grandstand
Face Value of tickets is $45

Section 11 is down the right field line behind Loge Box sections 98-100 and Field Box sections 9-10.

Section 11 borders Outfield Grandstand Section 10, where tickets have a face value of $27. This means that Section 11 is farther away from home plate than any other Infield Grandstand section on the first base side, and seats in Section 11 are much closer to the Pesky Pole than they are to first base.

Pole issues in Section 11 are fairly mild. If you are seated anywhere in the middle of the section you will have a clear view.

The view from the center of Section 11

Section II

ROW																					ROW
17	1	2	3	4	5	6	7	8	9	10	11	12	13	14	15	16	17	18	19	20	17
16	1	2	3	4	5	6	7	8	9	10	11	12	13	14	15	16	17	18	19	20	16
15	1	2	3	4	5	6	7	8	9	10	11	12	13	14	15	16	17	18	19	20	15
14	1	2	3	4	5	6	7	8	9	10	11	12	13	14	15	16	17	18	19	20	14
13	1	2	3	4	5	6	7	8	9	10	11	12	13	14	15	16	17	18	19	20	13
12	1	2	3	4	5	6	7	8	9	10	11	12	13	14	15	16	17	18	19	20	12
11	1	2	3	4	5	6	7	8	9	10	11	12	13	14	15	16	17	18	19	20	11
10	1	2	3	4	5	6	7	8	9	10	11	12	13	14	15	16	17	18	19	20	10
9	1	2	3	4	5	6	7	8	9	10	11	12	13	14	15	16	17	18	19	20	9
8	1	2	3	4	5	6	7	8	9	10	11	12	13	14	15	16	17	18	19	20	8
7	1	2	3	4	5	6	7	8	9	10	11	12	13	14	15	16	17	18	19	20	7
6	1	2	3	4	5	6	7	8	9	10	11	12	13	14	15	16	17	18	19	20	6
5	1	2	3	4	5	6	7	8	9	10	11	12	13	14	15	16	17	18	19	20	5
4	1	2	3	4	5	6	7	8	9	10	11	12	13	14	15	16	17	18	19	20	4
3	1	2	3	4	5	6	7	8	9	10	11	12	13	14	15	16	17	18	19	20	3
2	1	2	3	4	5	6	7	8	9	10	11	12	13	14	15	16	17	18	19	20	2
1	1	2	3	4	5	6	7	8	9	10	11	12	13	14	15	16	17	18	19	20	1

= View of home plate or pitcher's mound is obstructed

Section 12

Infield Grandstand
Face Value of tickets is $45

Section 12 is down the right field line behind Loge Box sections 101-104 and Field Box sections 11-15.

Pole issues in Section 12 are confined to the right side of the section if you are facing the field. Any seat with a number of 15 or higher is safe from poles.

The view from the center of Section 12

Section 12

ROW																										ROW
17	1	2	3	4	5	6	7	8	9	10	11	12	13	14	15	16	17	18	19	20	21	22	23	24		17
16	1	2	3	4	5	6	7	8	9	10	11	12	13	14	15	16	17	18	19	20	21	22	23	24	25	16
15	1	2	3	4	5	6	7	8	9	10	11	12	13	14	15	16	17	18	19	20	21	22	23	24	25	15
14	1	2	3	4	5	6	7	8	9	10	11	12	13	14	15	16	17	18	19	20	21	22	23	24	25	14
13	1	2	3	4	5	6	7	8	9	10	11	12	13	14	15	16	17	18	19	20	21	22	23	24	25	13
12	1	2	3	4	5	6	7	8	9	10	11	12	13	14	15	16	17	18	19	20	21	22	23	24	25	12
11	1	2	3	4	5	6	7	8	9	10	11	12	13	14	15	16	17	18	19	20	21	22	23	24	25	11
10	1	2	3	4	5	6	7	8	9	10	11	12	13	14	15	16	17	18	19	20	21	22	23	24	25	10
9	1	2	3	4	5	6	7	8	9	10	11	12	13	14	15	16	17	18	19	20	21	22	23	24	25	9
8	1	2	3	4	5	6	7	8	9	10	11	12	13	14	15	16	17	18	19	20	21	22	23	24	25	8
7	1	2	3	4	5	6	7	8	9	10	11	12	13	14	15	16	17	18	19	20	21	22	23	24	25	7
6	1	2	3	4	5	6	7	8	9	10	11	12	13	14	15	16	17	18	19	20	21	22	23	24	25	6
5	1	2	3	4	5	6	7	8	9	10	11	12	13	14	15	16	17	18	19	20	21	22	23	24	25	5
4	1	2	3	4	5	6	7	8	9	10	11	12	13	14	15	16	17	18	19	20	21	22	23	24	25	4
3	1	2	3	4	5	6	7	8	9	10	11	12	13	14	15	16	17	18	19	20	21	22	23	24	25	3
2	1	2	3	4	5	6	7	8	9	10	11	12	13	14	15	16	17	18	19	20	21	22	23	24	25	2
1	1	2	3	4	5	6	7	8	9	10	11	12	13	14	15	16	17	18	19	20	21	22	23	24	25	1

= View of home plate or pitcher's mound is obstructed

home plate

Section 13

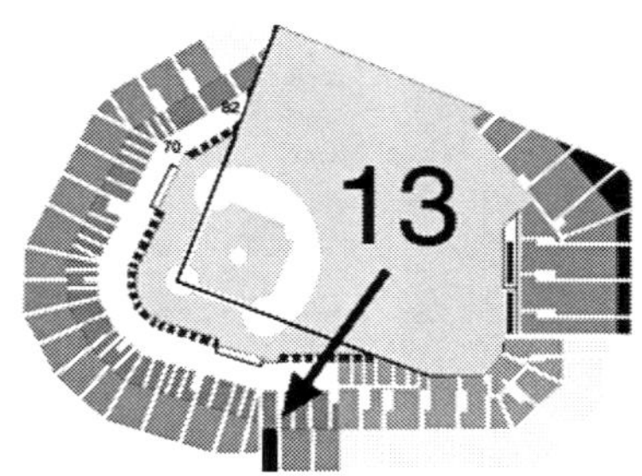

Infield Grandstand
Face Value of tickets is $45

Section 13 is down the first base line behind Loge Box section 105 and Field Box section 19.

Of all 33 Grandstand sections, 13 is one of the smallest. Only 12 seats wide on the bottom, it gradually narrows to 6 seats in the last 4 rows.

Pole issues in Section 13 run right down the middle of the section. If you are sitting in the middle of the section you will see a pole between home plate and the pitcher's mound. If you are sitting on the left or right side of the section, there is a good chance the pole will impede your view of home plate or the pitcher's mound.

The view from the center of Section 13

Section 13

ROW													ROW
16	1	2	3	4	5	6							16
15	1	2	3	4	5	6							15
14	1	2	3	4	5	6							14
13	1	2	3	4	5	6							13
12	1	2	3	4	5	6	7						12
11	1	2	3	4	5	6	7	8					11
10	1	2	3	4	5	6	7	8	9	10			10
9	1	2	3	4	5	6	7	8	9	10	11		9
8	1	2	3	4	5	6	7	8	9	10	11		8
7	1	2	3	4	5	6	7	8	9	10	11		7
6	1	2	3	4	5	6	7	8	9	10	11	12	6
5	1	2	3	4	5	6	7	8	9	10	11	12	5
4	1	2	3	4	5	6	7	8	9	10	11	12	4
3	1	2	3	4	5	6	7	8	9	10	11	12	3
2	1	2	3	4	5	6	7	8	9	10	11	12	2
1	1	2	3	4	5	6	7	8	9	10	11	12	1

= View of home plate or pitcher's mound is obstructed

home plate

Section 14

Infield Grandstand
Face Value of tickets is $45

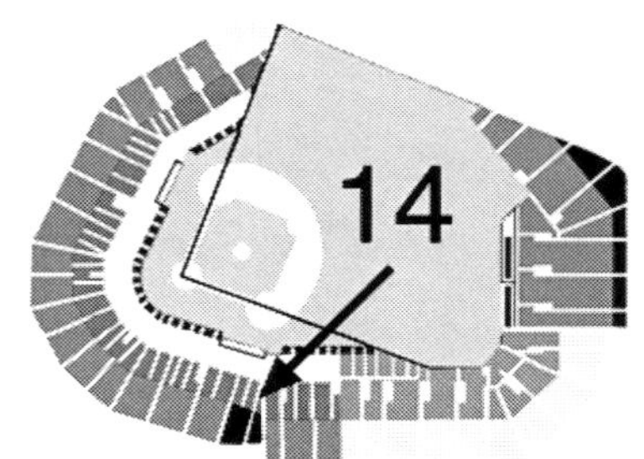

Section 14 is down the first base line behind Loge Boxes 106-110 and Field Boxes 20-23.

It is located behind first base and the home dugout, and an aisle runs down the middle of the section. Because of the aisle you may have seats that are numbered consecutively but are actually across the aisle from one another.

Pole issues in Section 14 are limited to the left side of the section if you are facing the field. If you are seated anywhere to the right of the aisle you will have a clear view.

The view from the center of Section 14

Section 14

ROW	Seats	AISLE	Seats	ROW
15	1		2 3 4 5 6 7 8 9 10 11 12 13 14 15 16	15
14	1 2 3 4 5 6 7 8		9 10 11 12 13 14 15 16 17 18 19 20 21 22 23	14
13	1 2 3 4 5 6 7 8 9 10 11		12 13 14 15 16 17 18 19 20 21 22 23 24 25 26	13
12	1 2 3 4 5 6 7 8 9 10 11 12 13 14		15 16 17 18 19 20 21 22 23 24 25 26 27 28 29	12
11	1 2 3 4 5 6 7 8 9 10 11 12 13 14		15 16 17 18 19 20 21 22 23 24 25 26 27 28 29	11
10	1 2 3 4 5 6 7 8 9 10 11 12 13 14		15 16 17 18 19 20 21 22 23 24 25 26 27 28 29	10
9	1 2 3 4 5 6 7 8 9 10 11 12 13		14 15 16 17 18 19 20 21 22 23 24 25 26 27 28	9
8	1 2 3 4 5 6 7 8 9 10 11 12 13		14 15 16 17 18 19 20 21 22 23 24 25 26 27 28	8
7	1 2 3 4 5 6 7 8 9 10 11 12 13		14 15 16 17 18 19 20 21 22 23 24 25 26 27 28	7
6	1 2 3 4 5 6 7 8 9 10 11 12		13 14 15 16 17 18 19 20 21 22 23 24 25 26 27	6
5	1 2 3 4 5 6 7 8 9 10 11 12		13 14 15 16 17 18 19 20 21 22 23 24 25 26 27	5
4	1 2 3 4 5 6 7 8 9 10 11		12 13 14 15 16 17 18 19 20 21 22 23 24 25 26	4
3	1 2 3 4 5 6 7 8 9 10 11		12 13 14 15 16 17 18 19 20 21 22 23 24 25 26	3
2	1 2 3 4 5 6 7 8 9 10		11 12 13 14 15 16 17 18 19 20 21 22 23 24 25	2
1	1 2 3 4 5 6 7 8 9		10 11 12 13 14 15 16 17 18 19 20 21 22 23 24	1

home plate

= View of home plate or pitcher's mound is obstructed

Section 15

Infield Grandstand
Face Value of tickets is $45

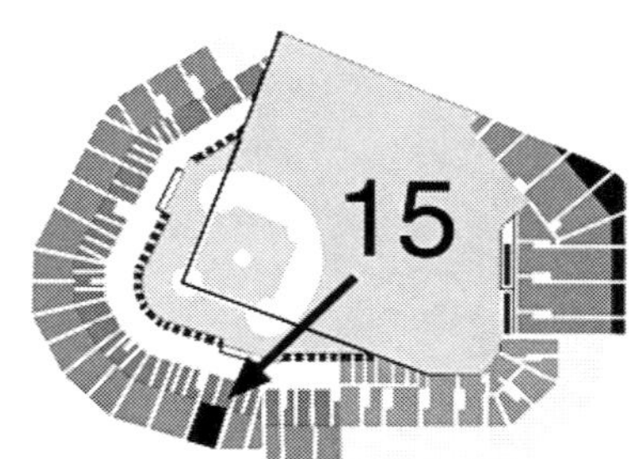

Section 15 is down the first base line behind Loge Boxes 111-114 and Field Boxes 24-28.

It is located in between home plate and first base and provides an excellent view of the field and the entire park.

Pole issues are limited to the left side of the section if you are facing the field.

The view from the center of Section 15

Section 15

	19	1	2	3	4	5	6	7	8	9	10	11	12	13	14	15	16	17	18	19	20	21	22	23	24	19	
	18	1	2	3	4	5	6	7	8	9	10	11	12	13	14	15	16	17	18	19	20	21	22	23	24	18	
	17	1	2	3	4	5	6	7	8	9	10	11	12	13	14	15	16	17	18	19	20	21	22	23	24	17	
	16		1	2	3	4	5	6	7	8	9	10	11	12	13	14	15	16	17	18	19	20	21	22	23	16	
	15		1	2	3	4	5	6	7	8	9	10	11	12	13	14	15	16	17	18	19	20	21	22	23	15	
	14	1	2	3	4	5	6	7	8	9	10	11	12	13	14	15	16	17	18	19	20	21	22	23	24	14	
	13	1	2	3	4	5	6	7	8	9	10	11	12	13	14	15	16	17	18	19	20	21	22	23	24	13	
	12	1	2	3	4	5	6	7	8	9	10	11	12	13	14	15	16	17	18	19	20	21	22	23	24	12	
R	11	1	2	3	4	5	6	7	8	9	10	11	12	13	14	15	16	17	18	19	20	21	22	23	24	11	R
O	10	1	2	3	4	5	6	7	8	9	10	11	12	13	14	15	16	17	18	19	20	21	22	23	24	10	O
W	9	1	2	3	4	5	6	7	8	9	10	11	12	13	14	15	16	17	18	19	20	21	22	23	24	9	W
	8	1	2	3	4	5	6	7	8	9	10	11	12	13	14	15	16	17	18	19	20	21	22	23	24	8	
	7	1	2	3	4	5	6	7	8	9	10	11	12	13	14	15	16	17	18	19	20	21	22	23	24	7	
	6	1	2	3	4	5	6	7	8	9	10	11	12	13	14	15	16	17	18	19	20	21	22	23	24	6	
	5	1	2	3	4	5	6	7	8	9	10	11	12	13	14	15	16	17	18	19	20	21	22	23	24	5	
	4	1	2	3	4	5	6	7	8	9	10	11	12	13	14	15	16	17	18	19	20	21	22	23	24	4	
	3	1	2	3	4	5	6	7	8	9	10	11	12	13	14	15	16	17	18	19	20	21	22	23	24	3	
	2	1	2	3	4	5	6	7	8	9	10	11	12	13	14	15	16	17	18	19	20	21	22	23	24	2	
	1		1	2	3	4	5	6	7	8	9	10	11	12	13	14	15	16	17	18	19	20	21	22	23	1	

 = View of home plate or pitcher's mound is obstructed

home plate

Section 16

Infield Grandstand
Face Value of tickets is $45

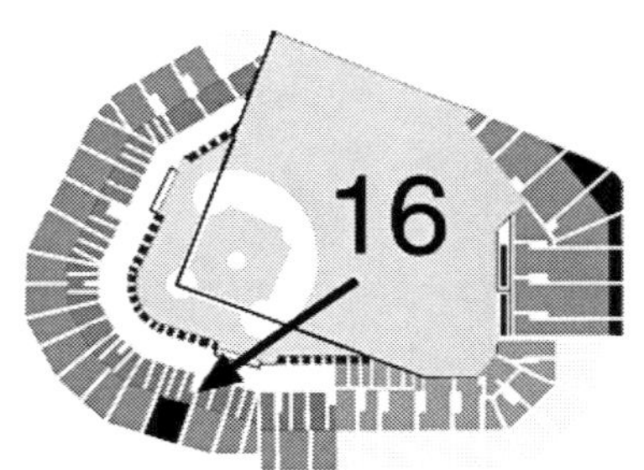

Section 16 is on the first base line behind Loge Boxes 115-118 and Field Boxes 29-32.

It is located in between home plate and first base and provides an excellent view of the field and the entire park.

Pole issues are limited to the left side of the section if you are facing the field.

The view from the center of Section 16

Section 16

ROW																											ROW
19			1	2	3	4	5	6	7	8	9	10	11	12	13	14	15	16	17	18	19	20	21	22	23	24	19
18			1	2	3	4	5	6	7	8	9	10	11	12	13	14	15	16	17	18	19	20	21	22	23	24	18
17			1	2	3	4	5	6	7	8	9	10	11	12	13	14	15	16	17	18	19	20	21	22	23	24	17
16	1	2	3	4	5	6	7	8	9	10	11	12	13	14	15	16	17	18	19	20	21	22	23	24	25	26	16
15	1	2	3	4	5	6	7	8	9	10	11	12	13	14	15	16	17	18	19	20	21	22	23	24	25	26	15
14	1	2	3	4	5	6	7	8	9	10	11	12	13	14	15	16	17	18	19	20	21	22	23	24	25	26	14
13	1	2	3	4	5	6	7	8	9	10	11	12	13	14	15	16	17	18	19	20	21	22	23	24	25	26	13
12	1	2	3	4	5	6	7	8	9	10	11	12	13	14	15	16	17	18	19	20	21	22	23	24	25	26	12
11	1	2	3	4	5	6	7	8	9	10	11	12	13	14	15	16	17	18	19	20	21	22	23	24	25	26	11
10	1	2	3	4	5	6	7	8	9	10	11	12	13	14	15	16	17	18	19	20	21	22	23	24	25	26	10
9	1	2	3	4	5	6	7	8	9	10	11	12	13	14	15	16	17	18	19	20	21	22	23	24	25	26	9
8	1	2	3	4	5	6	7	8	9	10	11	12	13	14	15	16	17	18	19	20	21	22	23	24	25	26	8
7	1	2	3	4	5	6	7	8	9	10	11	12	13	14	15	16	17	18	19	20	21	22	23	24	25	26	7
6	1	2	3	4	5	6	7	8	9	10	11	12	13	14	15	16	17	18	19	20	21	22	23	24	25	26	6
5	1	2	3	4	5	6	7	8	9	10	11	12	13	14	15	16	17	18	19	20	21	22	23	24	25	26	5
4	1	2	3	4	5	6	7	8	9	10	11	12	13	14	15	16	17	18	19	20	21	22	23	24	25	26	4
3	1	2	3	4	5	6	7	8	9	10	11	12	13	14	15	16	17	18	19	20	21	22	23	24	25	26	3
2	1	2	3	4	5	6	7	8	9	10	11	12	13	14	15	16	17	18	19	20	21	22	23	24	25	26	2
1	1	2	3	4	5	6	7	8	9	10	11	12	13	14	15	16	17	18	19	20	21	22	23	24	25	26	1

= View of home plate or pitcher's mound is obstructed

home plate

Section 17

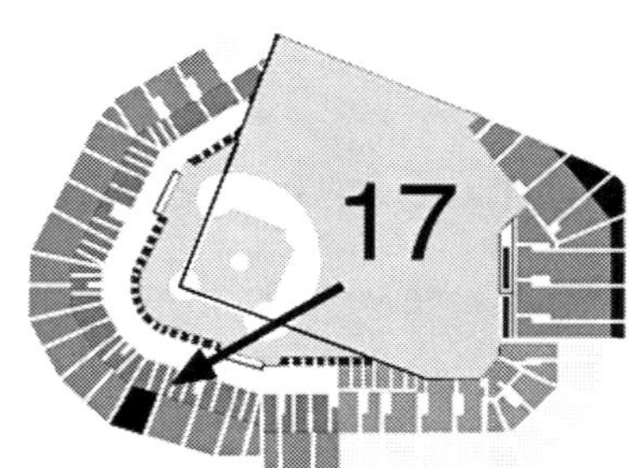

Infield Grandstand
Face Value of tickets is $45

Section 17 is near the Sox on deck circle behind Loge Boxes 119-122 and Field Boxes 33-36.

The view from the center of the section is straight down the third base line. It is one of the better sections to sit in, because there are very few seats with pole issues and there are also no home plate screen issues.

Pole issues are limited to a few seats on the right side of the section if you are facing the field.

The view from the center of Section 17

Section 17

ROW
ROW
= View of home plate or pitcher's mound is obstructed
home plate

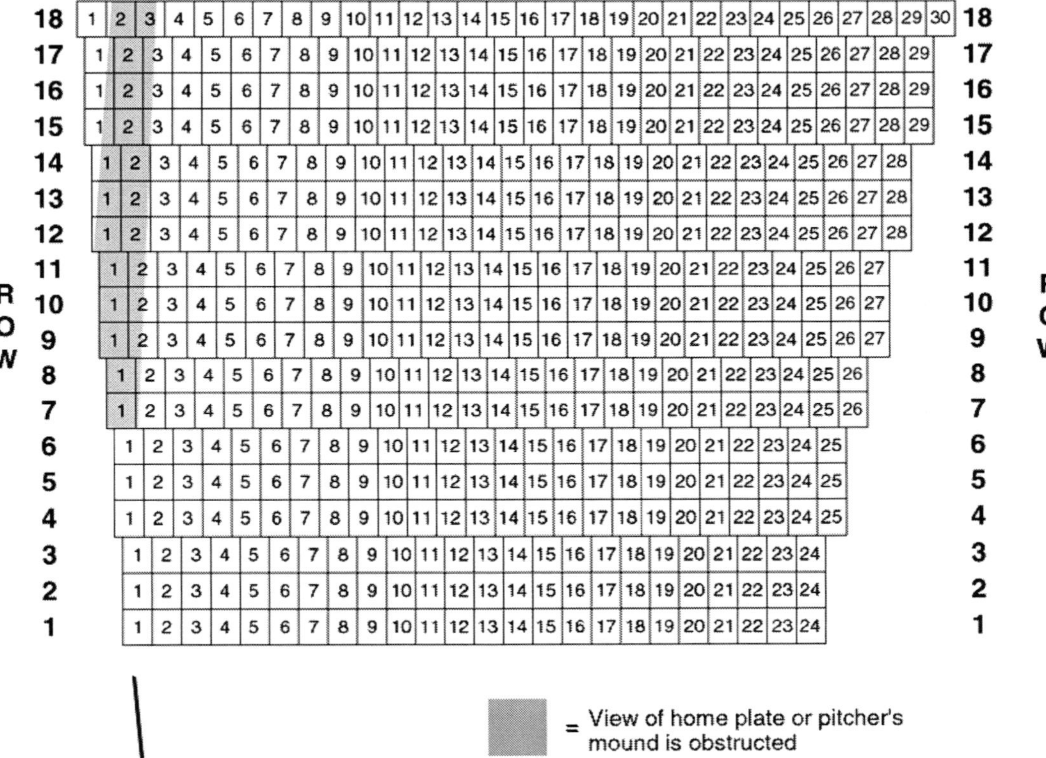

Section 18

Infield Grandstand
Face Value of tickets is $45

Section 18 is near home plate behind Loge Boxes 123-125 and Field Boxes 38-40.

The vast majority of the seats in this section are very good, as they can rightly be described as being "behind home plate." Some of the seats on the left side of the section facing the field have the home plate foul ball screen to look through, which can be a minor annoyance.

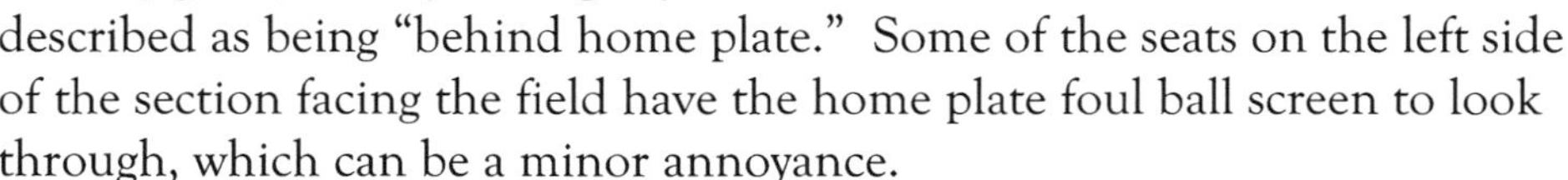

There is a pole that obstructs the view of seats 4, 5, 6, or 7 in most of the rows.

The view from the center of Section 18

Section 18

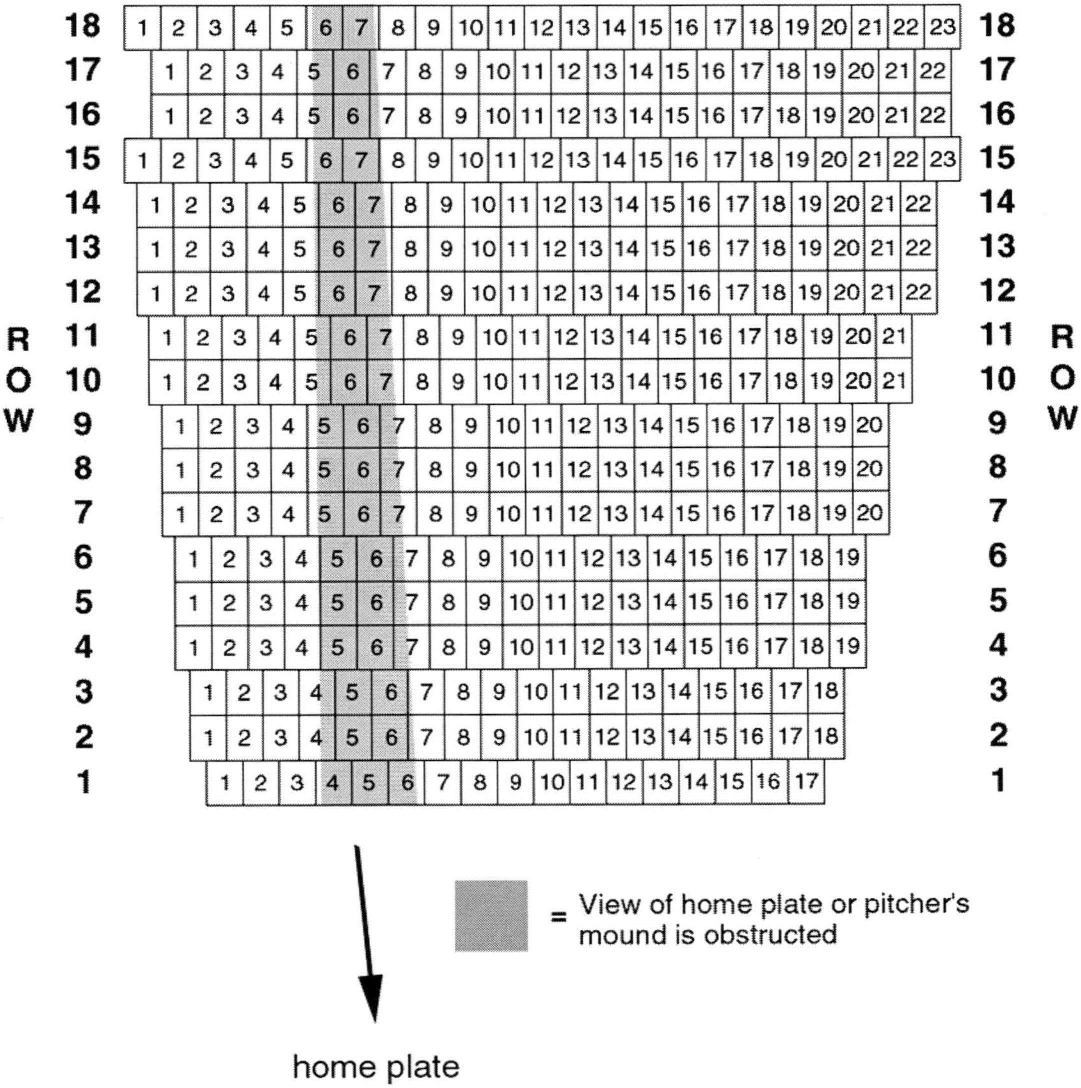

ROW																								ROW
18	1	2	3	4	5	6	7	8	9	10	11	12	13	14	15	16	17	18	19	20	21	22	23	18
17	1	2	3	4	5	6	7	8	9	10	11	12	13	14	15	16	17	18	19	20	21	22		17
16	1	2	3	4	5	6	7	8	9	10	11	12	13	14	15	16	17	18	19	20	21	22		16
15	1	2	3	4	5	6	7	8	9	10	11	12	13	14	15	16	17	18	19	20	21	22	23	15
14	1	2	3	4	5	6	7	8	9	10	11	12	13	14	15	16	17	18	19	20	21	22		14
13	1	2	3	4	5	6	7	8	9	10	11	12	13	14	15	16	17	18	19	20	21	22		13
12	1	2	3	4	5	6	7	8	9	10	11	12	13	14	15	16	17	18	19	20	21	22		12
11	1	2	3	4	5	6	7	8	9	10	11	12	13	14	15	16	17	18	19	20	21			11
10	1	2	3	4	5	6	7	8	9	10	11	12	13	14	15	16	17	18	19	20	21			10
9	1	2	3	4	5	6	7	8	9	10	11	12	13	14	15	16	17	18	19	20				9
8	1	2	3	4	5	6	7	8	9	10	11	12	13	14	15	16	17	18	19	20				8
7	1	2	3	4	5	6	7	8	9	10	11	12	13	14	15	16	17	18	19	20				7
6	1	2	3	4	5	6	7	8	9	10	11	12	13	14	15	16	17	18	19					6
5	1	2	3	4	5	6	7	8	9	10	11	12	13	14	15	16	17	18	19					5
4	1	2	3	4	5	6	7	8	9	10	11	12	13	14	15	16	17	18	19					4
3	1	2	3	4	5	6	7	8	9	10	11	12	13	14	15	16	17	18						3
2	1	2	3	4	5	6	7	8	9	10	11	12	13	14	15	16	17	18						2
1	1	2	3	4	5	6	7	8	9	10	11	12	13	14	15	16	17							1

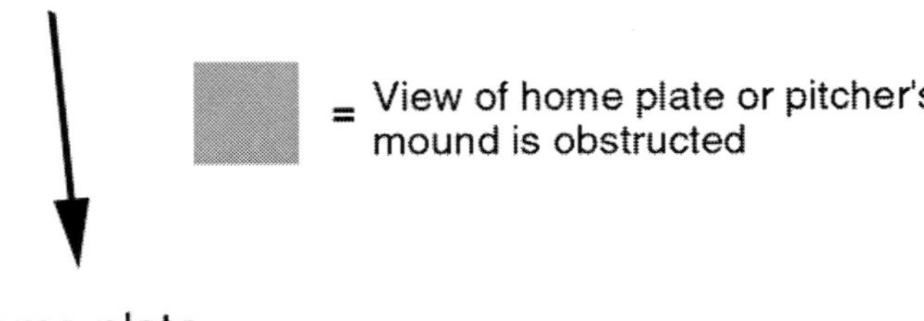

home plate

Section 19

Infield Grandstand
Face Value of tickets is $45

Section 19 is near home plate behind Loge Boxes 126-128 and Field Boxes 40-41.

Section 19 is one of the best sections in the entire park. Gloriously free from any pole obstructions, it is behind home plate and offers a great view of everything. The only minor annoyance could be looking through the foul ball screen.

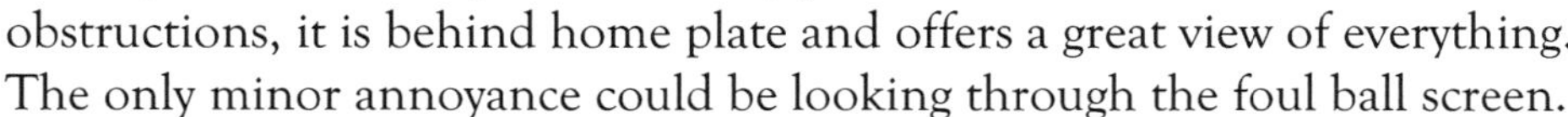

There are no pole issues in Section 19. Along with Section 21, it is one of only two Grandstand Sections in the park completely unaffected by poles.

The view from the center of Section 19

Section 19

ROW																								ROW
18	1	2	3	4	5	6	7	8	9	10	11	12	13	14	15	16	17	18	19	20	21	22	23	18
17	1	2	3	4	5	6	7	8	9	10	11	12	13	14	15	16	17	18	19	20	21	22	23	17
16	1	2	3	4	5	6	7	8	9	10	11	12	13	14	15	16	17	18	19	20	21	22	23	16
15	1	2	3	4	5	6	7	8	9	10	11	12	13	14	15	16	17	18	19	20	21	22		15
14	1	2	3	4	5	6	7	8	9	10	11	12	13	14	15	16	17	18	19	20	21	22		14
13	1	2	3	4	5	6	7	8	9	10	11	12	13	14	15	16	17	18	19	20	21			13
12	1	2	3	4	5	6	7	8	9	10	11	12	13	14	15	16	17	18	19	20	21			12
11	1	2	3	4	5	6	7	8	9	10	11	12	13	14	15	16	17	18	19	20				11
10	1	2	3	4	5	6	7	8	9	10	11	12	13	14	15	16	17	18	19	20				10
9	1	2	3	4	5	6	7	8	9	10	11	12	13	14	15	16	17	18	19					9
8	1	2	3	4	5	6	7	8	9	10	11	12	13	14	15	16	17	18	19					8
7	1	2	3	4	5	6	7	8	9	10	11	12	13	14	15	16	17	18	19					7
6	1	2	3	4	5	6	7	8	9	10	11	12	13	14	15	16	17	18						6
5	1	2	3	4	5	6	7	8	9	10	11	12	13	14	15	16	17	18						5
4	1	2	3	4	5	6	7	8	9	10	11	12	13	14	15	16	17	18						4
3	1	2	3	4	5	6	7	8	9	10	11	12	13	14	15	16	17							3
2	1	2	3	4	5	6	7	8	9	10	11	12	13	14	15	16	17							2
1	1	2	3	4	5	6	7	8	9	10	11	12	13	14	15	16	17							1

There are no pole obstructions in Section 19

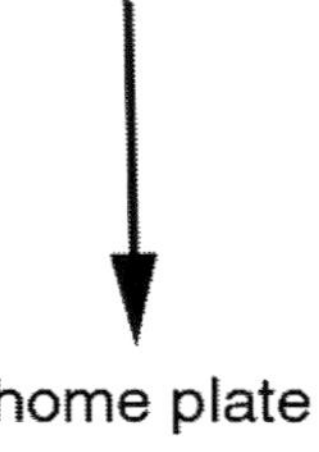

home plate

Section 20

Infield Grandstand
Face Value of tickets is $45

Section 20 is in back of home plate behind Loge Boxes 129-130 and Field Boxes 42-44.

Section 20 is one of the best sections in the entire park. It is behind home plate and offers a great view of everything. The only minor annoyance could be looking through the foul ball screen.

Pole issues in Section 20 are limited to seats 1 and 2 in rows 3 through 18. Any seat numbered 4 or higher is safe from poles.

The view from the center of Section 20

Section 20

ROW
ROW
= View of home plate or pitcher's mound is obstructed
home plate

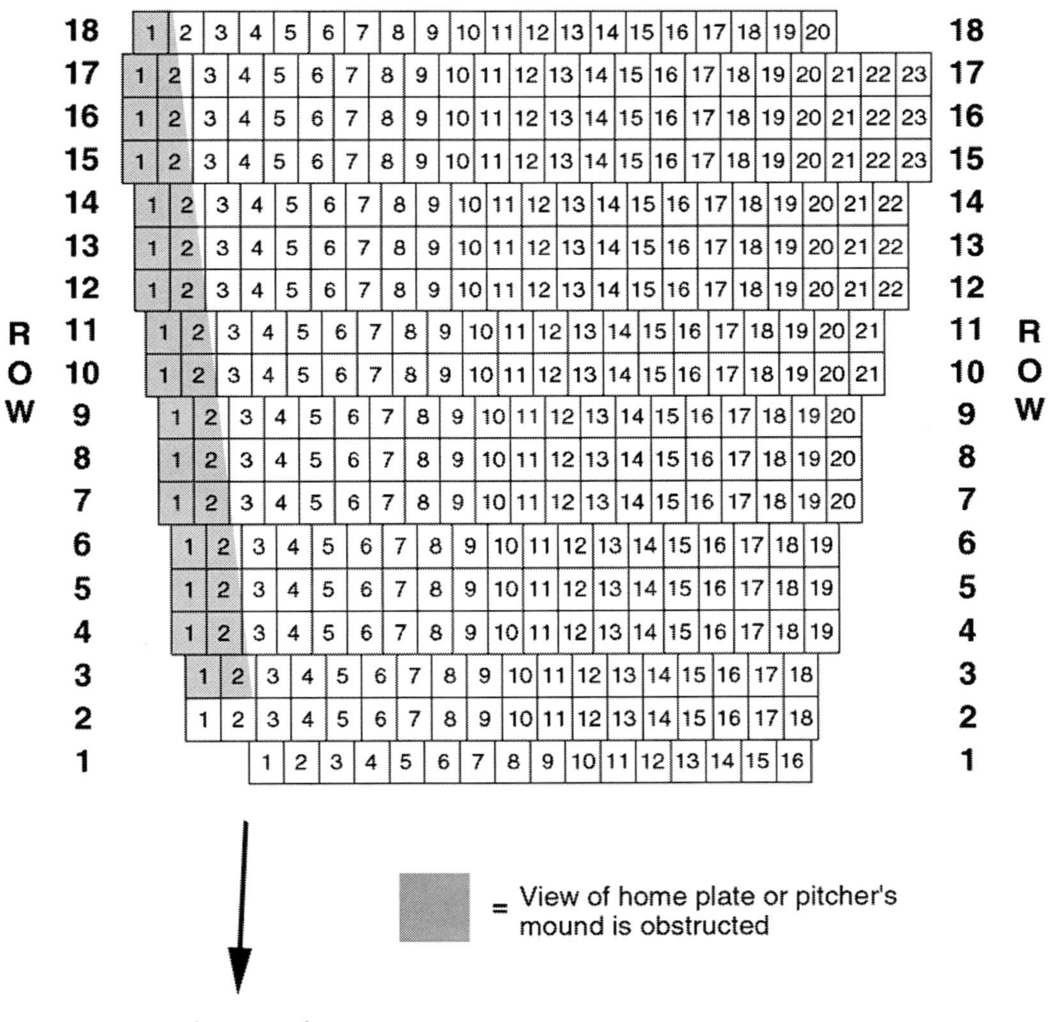

Section 21

Infield Grandstand
Face Value of tickets is $45

Section 21 is near home plate behind Loge Boxes 130-131 and Field Boxes 45-47.

Section 21 is one of the best sections in the entire park. Gloriously free from any pole obstructions, it is behind home plate and offers a great view of everything. The only minor annoyance could be looking through the foul ball screen.

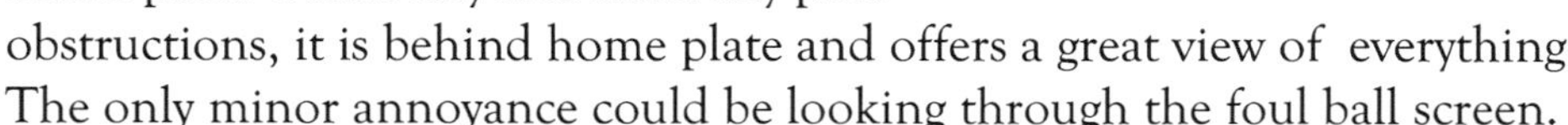

There are no pole issues in Section 21. Along with Section 19, it is one of only two Grandstand Sections in the park completely unaffected by poles.

The view from the center of Section 21

Section 21

ROW																								ROW
16	1	2	3	4	5	6	7	8	9	10	11	12	13	14	15	16	17	18	19	20	21	22	23	16
15	1	2	3	4	5	6	7	8	9	10	11	12	13	14	15	16	17	18	19	20	21	22	23	15
14	1	2	3	4	5	6	7	8	9	10	11	12	13	14	15	16	17	18	19	20	21	22		14
13	1	2	3	4	5	6	7	8	9	10	11	12	13	14	15	16	17	18	19	20	21	22		13
12	1	2	3	4	5	6	7	8	9	10	11	12	13	14	15	16	17	18	19	20	21			12
11	1	2	3	4	5	6	7	8	9	10	11	12	13	14	15	16	17	18	19	20	21			11
10	1	2	3	4	5	6	7	8	9	10	11	12	13	14	15	16	17	18	19	20	21			10
9	1	2	3	4	5	6	7	8	9	10	11	12	13	14	15	16	17	18	19	20				9
8	1	2	3	4	5	6	7	8	9	10	11	12	13	14	15	16	17	18	19	20				8
7	1	2	3	4	5	6	7	8	9	10	11	12	13	14	15	16	17	18	19	20				7
6	1	2	3	4	5	6	7	8	9	10	11	12	13	14	15	16	17	18	19					6
5	1	2	3	4	5	6	7	8	9	10	11	12	13	14	15	16	17	18	19					5
4	1	2	3	4	5	6	7	8	9	10	11	12	13	14	15	16	17	18						4
3	1	2	3	4	5	6	7	8	9	10	11	12	13	14	15	16	17	18						3
2	1	2	3	4	5	6	7	8	9	10	11	12	13	14	15	16	17	18						2
1	1	2	3	4	5	6	7	8	9	10	11	12	13	14	15	16	17							1

There are no pole obstructions in Section 21

home plate

Section 22

Infield Grandstand
Face Value of tickets is $45

Section 22 is in back of home plate behind Loge Boxes 132-134 and Field Boxes 48-49.

Section 22 is one of the better sections in the entire park. It is behind home plate on the third base side and offers a great view of everything. The only minor annoyance could be looking through the foul ball screen.

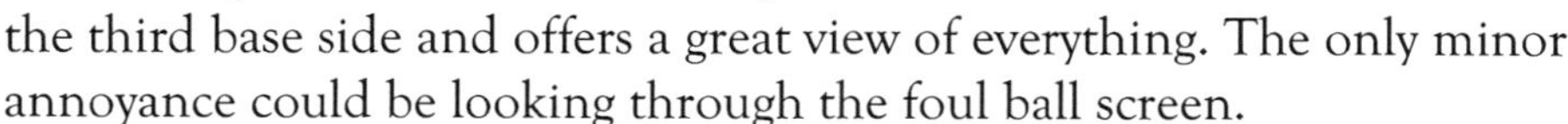

Pole issues in Section 22 are limited to seats 1 and, in come cases, 2 in rows 2 through 16. Any seat numbered 3 or higher is safe from poles.

The view from the center of Section 22

Section 22

ROW
ROW
16 15 14 13 12 11 10 9 8 7 6 5 4 3 2 1
home plate
= View of home plate or pitcher's mound is obstructed

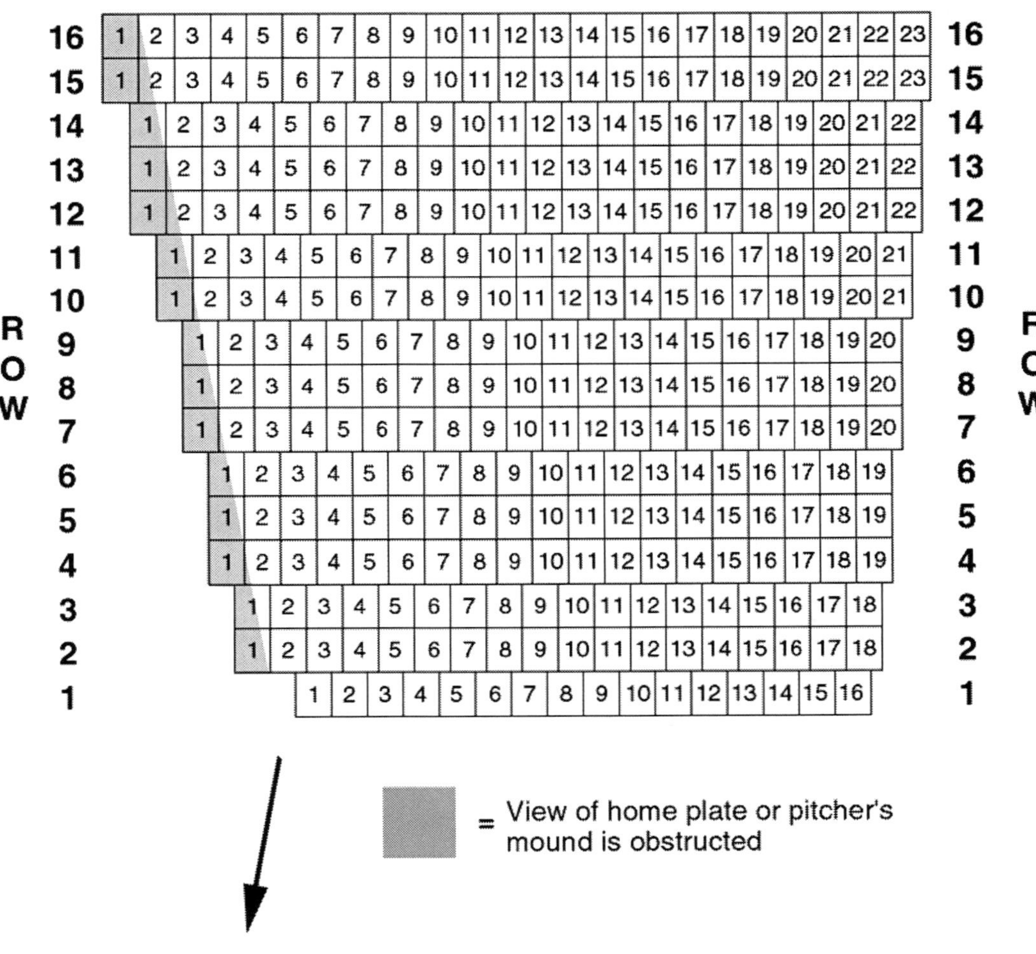

Section 23

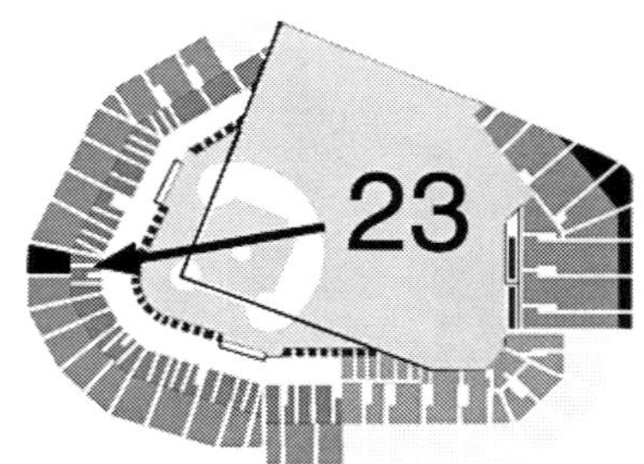

Infield Grandstand
Face Value of tickets is $45

Section 23 is near home plate and behind Loge Boxes 135-136 and Field Boxes 50-51.

Section 23 is an excellent section. It is near home plate and offers a great view of the entire park.

There is a pole which obstructs the view the higher numbered seats on the end of the rows. Any seat numbered 15 or lower is safe from poles.

The view from the center of Section 23

Section 23

ROW																								ROW
17	1	2	3	4	5	6	7	8	9	10	11	12	13	14	15	16	17	18	19	20	21	22	23	17
16	1	2	3	4	5	6	7	8	9	10	11	12	13	14	15	16	17	18	19	20	21	22		16
15	1	2	3	4	5	6	7	8	9	10	11	12	13	14	15	16	17	18	19	20	21	22	23	15
14	1	2	3	4	5	6	7	8	9	10	11	12	13	14	15	16	17	18	19	20	21	22		14
13	1	2	3	4	5	6	7	8	9	10	11	12	13	14	15	16	17	18	19	20	21	22		13
12	1	2	3	4	5	6	7	8	9	10	11	12	13	14	15	16	17	18	19	20	21			12
11	1	2	3	4	5	6	7	8	9	10	11	12	13	14	15	16	17	18	19	20	21			11
10	1	2	3	4	5	6	7	8	9	10	11	12	13	14	15	16	17	18	19	20	21			10
9	1	2	3	4	5	6	7	8	9	10	11	12	13	14	15	16	17	18	19	20				9
8	1	2	3	4	5	6	7	8	9	10	11	12	13	14	15	16	17	18	19	20				8
7	1	2	3	4	5	6	7	8	9	10	11	12	13	14	15	16	17	18	19	20				7
6	1	2	3	4	5	6	7	8	9	10	11	12	13	14	15	16	17	18	19					6
5	1	2	3	4	5	6	7	8	9	10	11	12	13	14	15	16	17	18	19					5
4	1	2	3	4	5	6	7	8	9	10	11	12	13	14	15	16	17	18						4
3	1	2	3	4	5	6	7	8	9	10	11	12	13	14	15	16	17	18						3
2	1	2	3	4	5	6	7	8	9	10	11	12	13	14	15	16	17	18						2
1	1	2	3	4	5	6	7	8	9	10	11	12	13	14	15	16								1

= View of home plate or pitcher's mound is obstructed

home plate

Section 24

Infield Grandstand
Face Value of tickets is $45

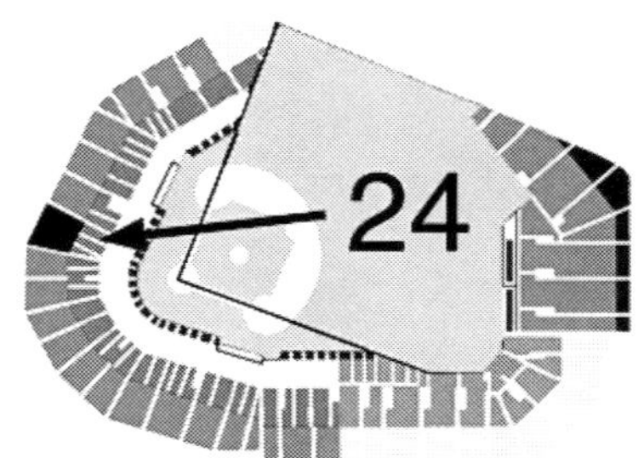

Section 24 is near the visiting team's on deck circle and behind Loge Boxes 137-140 and Field Boxes 51-55.

Section 24 is one of the best Grandstand sections in the park for viewing a game. Seats in the center of the section look directly down the first base line and are very close to the action.

Only a handful of seats in the upper rows at the very end of each row are affected by pole issues.

The view from the center of Section 24

Section 24

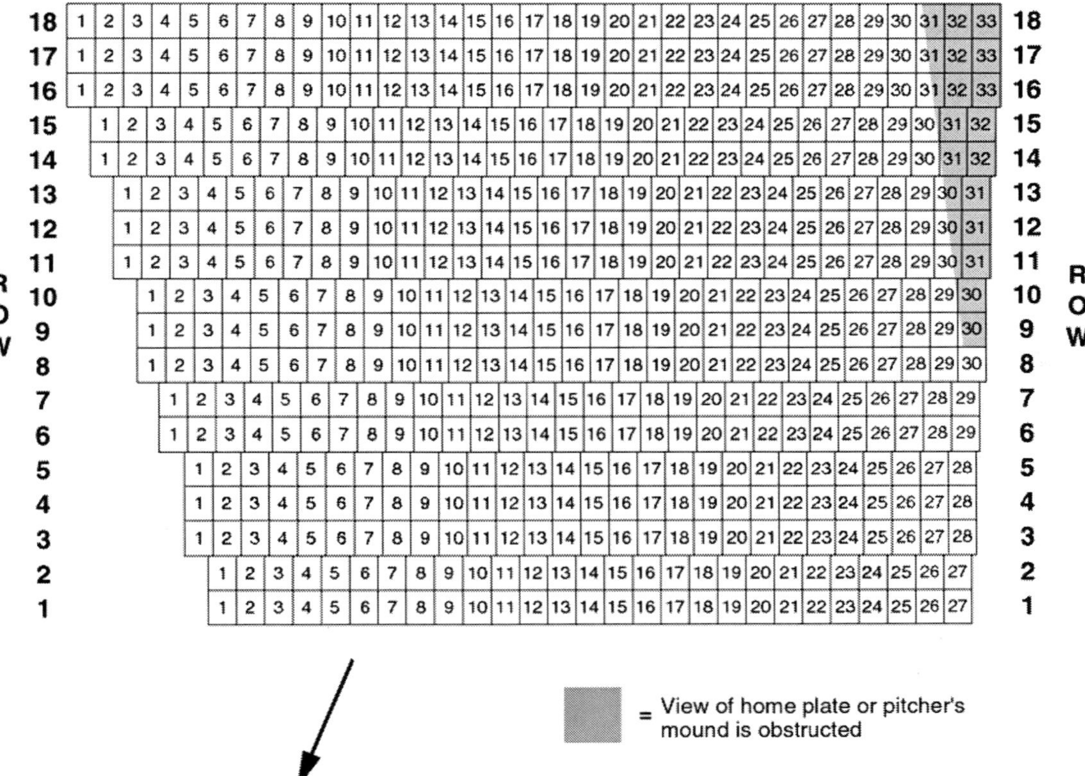

home plate

Section 25

Infield Grandstand
Face Value of tickets is $45

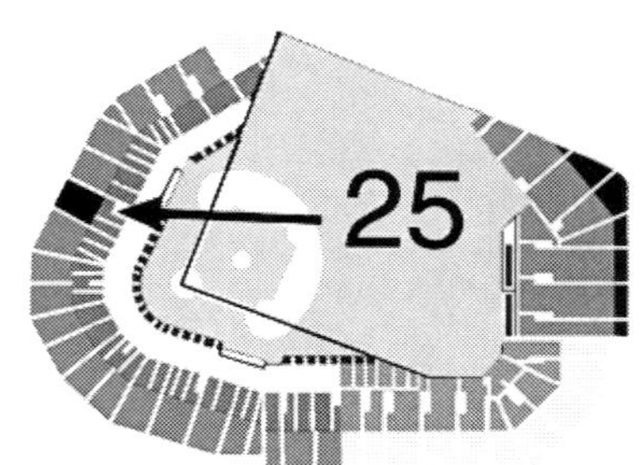

Section 25 is in between home plate and third base and behind Loge Boxes 141-144 and Field Boxes 56-60.

Section 25 is an excellent section for viewing the game. With the vast majority of the seats free from obstructions, you really have a nice view of the infield and the entire park from this section.

Only the first two seats in each row have pole issues.

The view from the center of Section 25

Section 25

ROW																									ROW
16		1	2	3	4	5	6	7	8	9	10	11	12	13	14	15	16	17	18	19	20	21	22	23	16
15	1	2	3	4	5	6	7	8	9	10	11	12	13	14	15	16	17	18	19	20	21	22	23	24	15
14	1	2	3	4	5	6	7	8	9	10	11	12	13	14	15	16	17	18	19	20	21	22	23	24	14
13	1	2	3	4	5	6	7	8	9	10	11	12	13	14	15	16	17	18	19	20	21	22	23	24	13
12	1	2	3	4	5	6	7	8	9	10	11	12	13	14	15	16	17	18	19	20	21	22	23	24	12
11	1	2	3	4	5	6	7	8	9	10	11	12	13	14	15	16	17	18	19	20	21	22	23	24	11
10	1	2	3	4	5	6	7	8	9	10	11	12	13	14	15	16	17	18	19	20	21	22	23	24	10
9	1	2	3	4	5	6	7	8	9	10	11	12	13	14	15	16	17	18	19	20	21	22	23	24	9
8	1	2	3	4	5	6	7	8	9	10	11	12	13	14	15	16	17	18	19	20	21	22	23	24	8
7	1	2	3	4	5	6	7	8	9	10	11	12	13	14	15	16	17	18	19	20	21	22	23	24	7
6	1	2	3	4	5	6	7	8	9	10	11	12	13	14	15	16	17	18	19	20	21	22	23	24	6
5	1	2	3	4	5	6	7	8	9	10	11	12	13	14	15	16	17	18	19	20	21	22	23	24	5
4	1	2	3	4	5	6	7	8	9	10	11	12	13	14	15	16	17	18	19	20	21	22	23	24	4
3	1	2	3	4	5	6	7	8	9	10	11	12	13	14	15	16	17	18	19	20	21	22	23	24	3
2	1	2	3	4	5	6	7	8	9	10	11	12	13	14	15	16	17	18	19	20	21	22	23	24	2
1		1	2	3	4	5	6	7	8	9	10	11	12	13	14	15	16	17	18	19	20	21	22	23	1

home plate

= View of home plate or pitcher's mound is obstructed

Section 26

Infield Grandstand
Face Value of tickets is $45

Section 26 is near third base and the visiting team's dugout. It is behind Loge Boxes 145-148 and Field Boxes 61-64.

Section 26 is a very good section for viewing the game. It is very close to the infield but also has a nice view of the Monster.

Pole issues in this section run diagonally from bottom right to seats in the middle of the top rows if you are facing the field. The pole issues in the first few rows with the lowest seat numbers are particularly problematic. The first two seats in rows 10 through 18 are also obstructed.

The view from the center of Section 26

Section 26

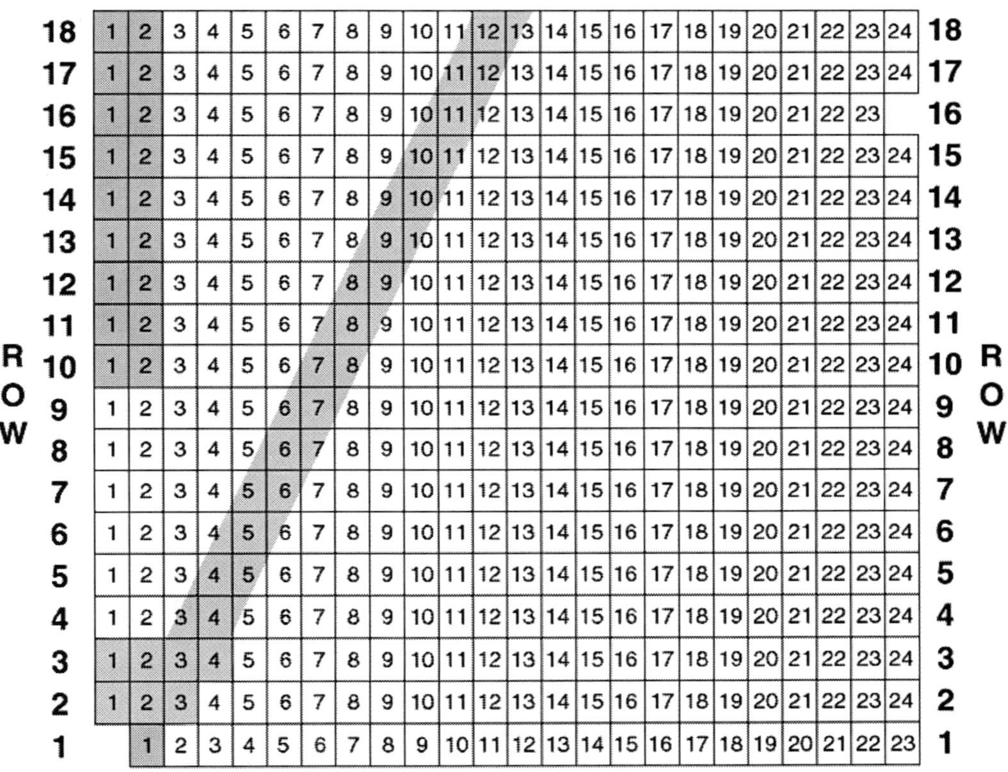

= View of home plate or pitcher's mound is obstructed

Section 27

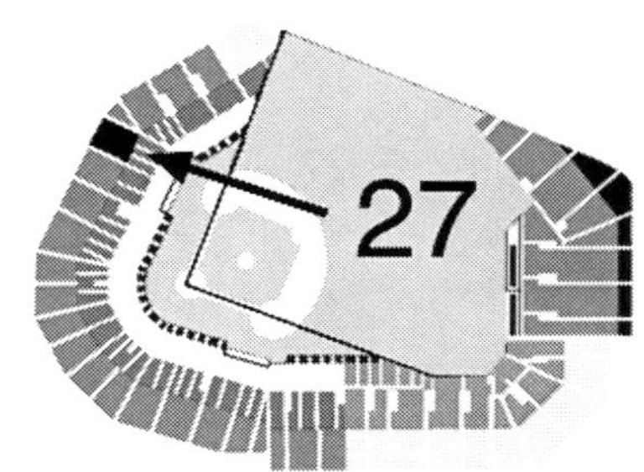

Infield Grandstand
Face Value of tickets is $45

Section 27 is just past third base on the left field line. It is behind Loge Boxes 149-151 and Field Boxes 65-68.

Section 27 is a very good section for viewing the game. It is close to the infield but also has a good view of the Monster.

Pole issues in this section run diagonally from bottom right to top left if you are facing the field. The pole issues in the first few rows with the lowest seat numbers are particularly problematic.

The view from the center of Section 27

Section 27

ROW																										ROW
18	1	2	3	4	5	6	7	8	9	10	11	12	13	14	15	16	17	18	19	20	21	22	23	24		18
17	1	2	3	4	5	6	7	8	9	10	11	12	13	14	15	16	17	18	19	20	21	22	23	24		17
16	1	2	3	4	5	6	7	8	9	10	11	12	13	14	15	16	17	18	19	20	21	22	23	24		16
15	1	2	3	4	5	6	7	8	9	10	11	12	13	14	15	16	17	18	19	20	21	22	23	24		15
14	1	2	3	4	5	6	7	8	9	10	11	12	13	14	15	16	17	18	19	20	21	22	23	24		14
13	1	2	3	4	5	6	7	8	9	10	11	12	13	14	15	16	17	18	19	20	21	22	23	24	25	13
12	1	2	3	4	5	6	7	8	9	10	11	12	13	14	15	16	17	18	19	20	21	22	23	24	25	12
11	1	2	3	4	5	6	7	8	9	10	11	12	13	14	15	16	17	18	19	20	21	22	23	24	25	11
10	1	2	3	4	5	6	7	8	9	10	11	12	13	14	15	16	17	18	19	20	21	22	23	24	25	10
9	1	2	3	4	5	6	7	8	9	10	11	12	13	14	15	16	17	18	19	20	21	22	23	24	25	9
8	1	2	3	4	5	6	7	8	9	10	11	12	13	14	15	16	17	18	19	20	21	22	23	24	25	8
7	1	2	3	4	5	6	7	8	9	10	11	12	13	14	15	16	17	18	19	20	21	22	23	24	25	7
6	1	2	3	4	5	6	7	8	9	10	11	12	13	14	15	16	17	18	19	20	21	22	23	24	25	6
5	1	2	3	4	5	6	7	8	9	10	11	12	13	14	15	16	17	18	19	20	21	22	23	24	25	5
4	1	2	3	4	5	6	7	8	9	10	11	12	13	14	15	16	17	18	19	20	21	22	23	24	25	4
3	1	2	3	4	5	6	7	8	9	10	11	12	13	14	15	16	17	18	19	20	21	22	23	24	25	3
2	1	2	3	4	5	6	7	8	9	10	11	12	13	14	15	16	17	18	19	20	21	22	23	24	25	2
1			1	2	3	4	5	6	7	8	9	10	11	12	13	14	15	16	17	18	19	20	21	22	23	1

home plate

= View of home plate or pitcher's mound is obstructed

Section 28

Infield Grandstand
Face Value of tickets is $45

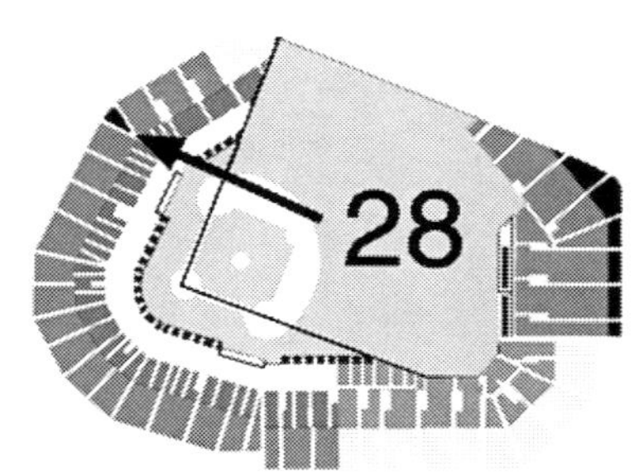

Section 28 is in just past third base on the left field line and is behind Loge Box 152 and Field Box 69.

Perhaps the most oddly shaped section in the park, 28 is basically a triangle. The first row is Row 3 and it has only one seat. The unusual shape is due to the fact that 28 is the junction between the sections that are parallel to the third base line (24-27) and the sections that turn so they can face the infield (29-33).

Pole issues are limited to upper row seats on the left and right sides of the section.

The view from the center of Section 28

Section 28

16
15
14
13
12
11
10
9
8
7
6
5
4
3
ROW
1 2 3 4 5 6 7 8 9 10
1 2 3 4 5 6 7 8 9 10 11
1 2 3 4 5 6 7 8 9 10 11 12 13
1 2 3 4 5 6 7 8 9 10 11 12
1 2 3 4 5 6 7 8 9 10 11
1 2 3 4 5 6 7 8 9 10
1 2 3 4 5 6 7 8 9
1 2 3 4 5 6 7 8
1 2 3 4 5 6 7
1 2 3 4 5 6
1 2 3 4 5
1 2 3 4
1 2 3
1

= View of home plate or pitcher's mound is obstructed
home plate

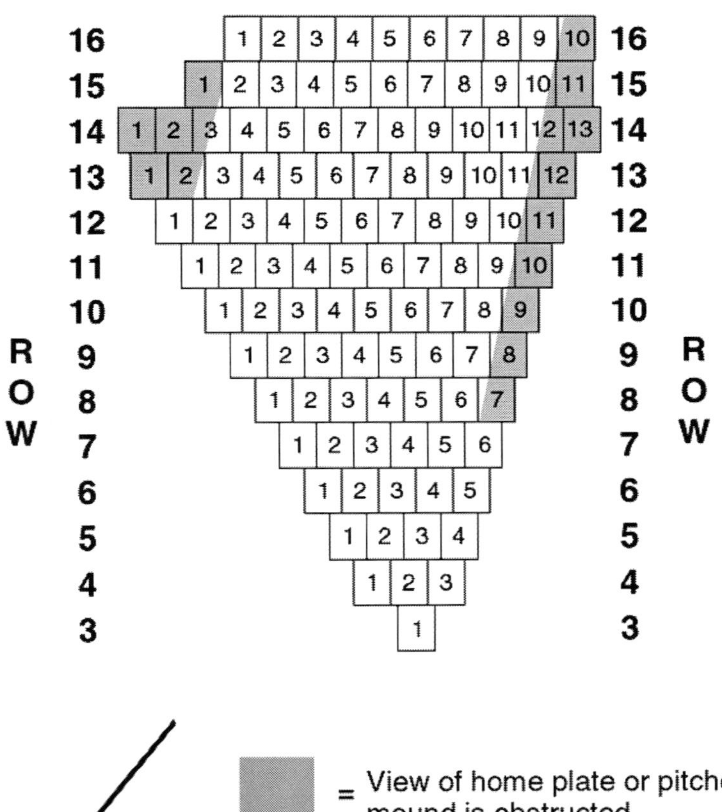

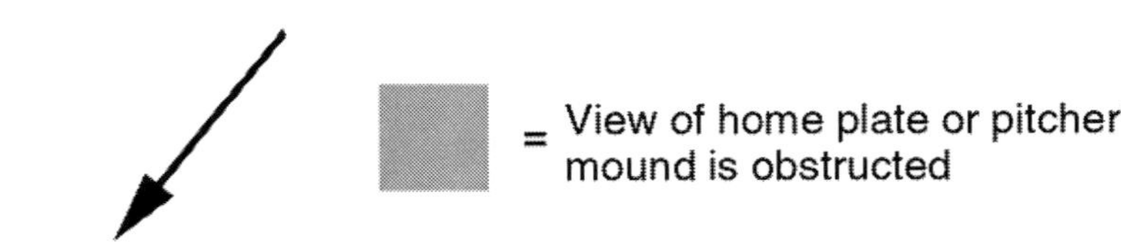

Section 29

Infield Grandstand
Face Value of tickets is $45

Section 29 is past third base on the left field line and is behind Loge Boxes 153-156 and Field Boxes 70-71.

It is an excellent section for viewing the game. The seats are close to the Green Monster and you are still fairly close to the infield.

A pole affects seats 1 and 2 in the first row and the obstruction runs diagonally up to seats 5 and 6 in row 18. The last seat in rows 3 and 4 are also affected.

The view from the center of Section 29

Section 29

16	1	2	3	4	**5**	**6**	7	8	9	10	11	12	13	14	15	16	17	18	19	20	21	22	23	24	25	26	16
15	1	2	3	4	**5**	6	7	8	9	10	11	12	13	14	15	16	17	18	19	20	21	22	23	24	25	26	15
14	1	2	3	4	**5**	6	7	8	9	10	11	12	13	14	15	16	17	18	19	20	21	22	23	24	25	26	14
13	1	2	3	**4**	**5**	6	7	8	9	10	11	12	13	14	15	16	17	18	19	20	21	22	23	24	25	26	13
12	1	2	3	**4**	**5**	6	7	8	9	10	11	12	13	14	15	16	17	18	19	20	21	22	23	24	25	26	12
11	1	2	3	**4**	5	6	7	8	9	10	11	12	13	14	15	16	17	18	19	20	21	22	23	24	25	26	11
ROW 10	1	2	**3**	**4**	5	6	7	8	9	10	11	12	13	14	15	16	17	18	19	20	21	22	23	24	25	26	10 ROW
9	1	2	**3**	**4**	5	6	7	8	9	10	11	12	13	14	15	16	17	18	19	20	21	22	23	24	25	26	9
8	1	2	**3**	4	5	6	7	8	9	10	11	12	13	14	15	16	17	18	19	20	21	22	23	24	25	26	8
7	1	2	**3**	4	5	6	7	8	9	10	11	12	13	14	15	16	17	18	19	20	21	22	23	24	25	26	7
6	1	**2**	**3**	4	5	6	7	8	9	10	11	12	13	14	15	16	17	18	19	20	21	22	23	24	25	26	6
5	1	**2**	**3**	4	5	6	7	8	9	10	11	12	13	14	15	16	17	18	19	20	21	22	23	24	25	26	5
4	1	**2**	3	4	5	6	7	8	9	10	11	12	13	14	15	16	17	18	19	20	21	22	23	24	25	**26**	4
3	1	**2**	3	4	5	6	7	8	9	10	11	12	13	14	15	16	17	18	19	20	21	22	23	24	25	**26**	3
2	**1**	**2**	3	4	5	6	7	8	9	10	11	12	13	14	15	16	17	18	19	20	21	22	23	24	25		2
1	**1**	**2**	3	4	5	6	7	8	9	10	11	12	13	14	15	16	17	18	19	20	21	22	23	24	25	26	1

home plate

= View of home plate or pitcher's mound is obstructed

Section 30

Infield Grandstand
Face Value of tickets is $45

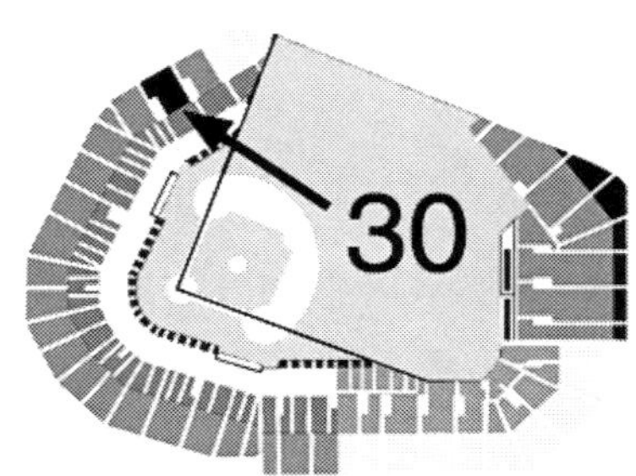

Section 30 is on the left field line between third base and the Green Monster and is behind Loge Boxes 157-159 and Field Boxes 72-76.

It is a very good section for viewing the game. The seats are close to the Green Monster and not too far from the infield.

Only a few seats have pole issues. If you are facing the field these are on the right side of the section in rows 8 through 15. Seat 19 in row 2 is also affected.

The view from the center of Section 30

Section 30

ROW
ROW
exit
ramp
home plate
= View of home plate or pitcher's mound is obstructed

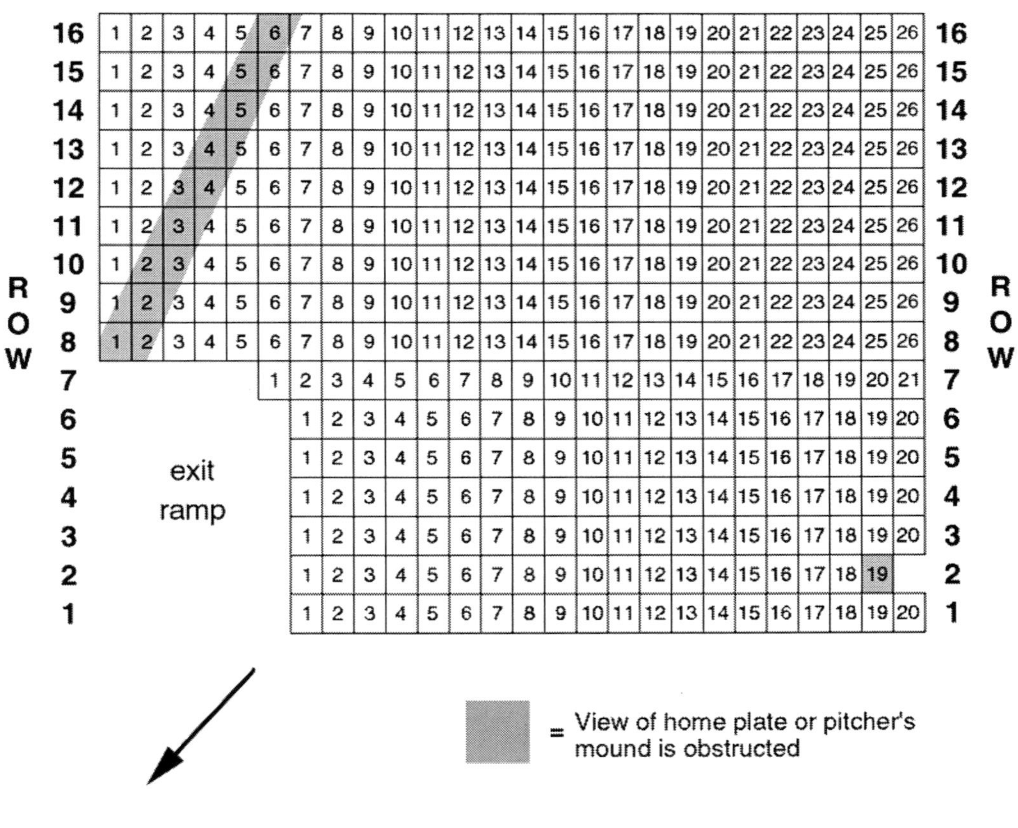

Section 31

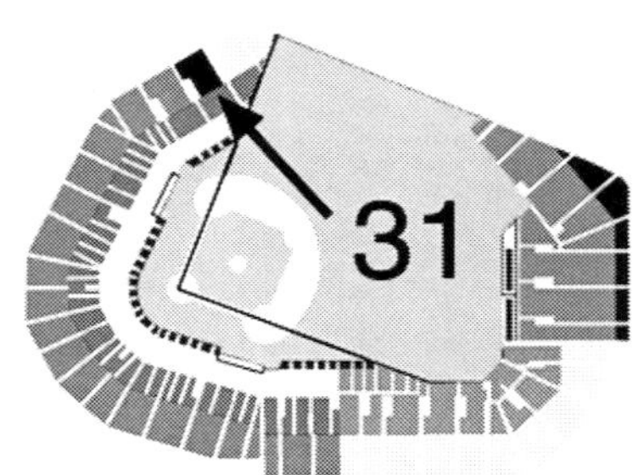

Infield Grandstand
Face Value of tickets is $45

Section 31 is on the left field line near the Green Monster and is behind Loge Boxes 160-161 and Field Boxes 77-82.

While it is a good section for viewing the game, be aware that it is further from home plate than any other section on the left side that is classified as Infield Grandstand. If you are one section over in Section 32, the face value of tickets drops to $27.

If you are facing the field, pole issues are limited to seats on the right in rows 8 through 16. All seats in the first 7 rows are not affected by poles, and in rows 8 through 16, any seats numbered higher than 11 are safe from poles.

The view from the center of Section 31

Section 31

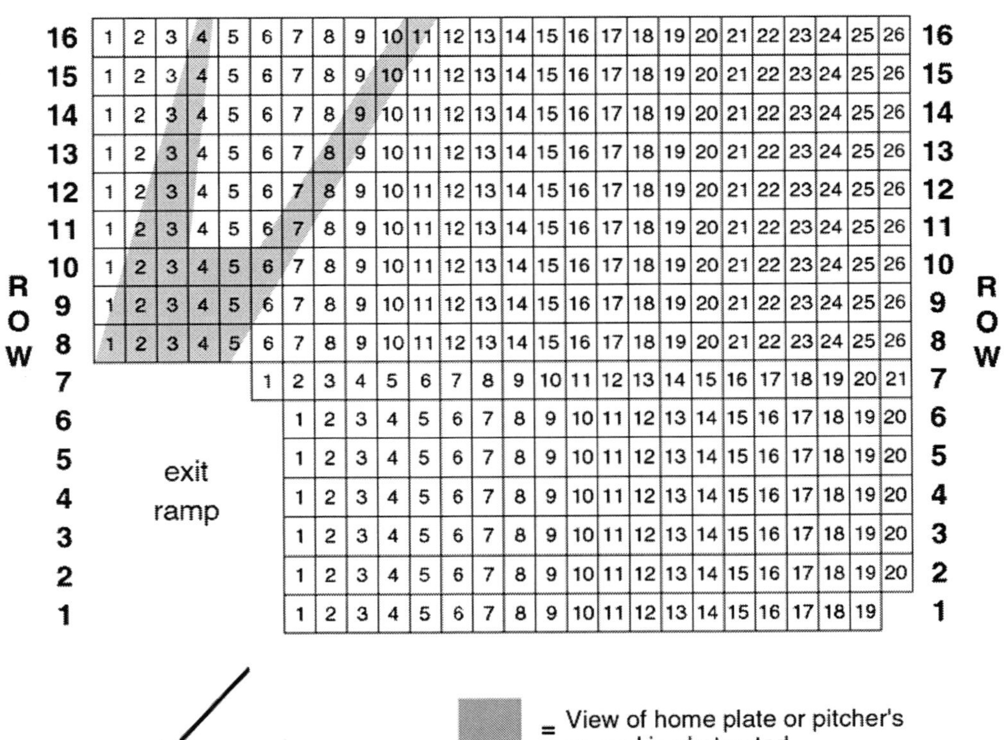

home plate

Section 32

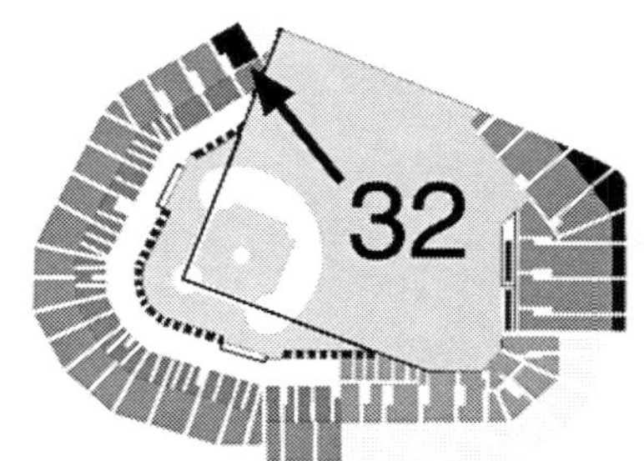

Outfield Grandstand
Face Value of tickets is $27
No alcohol section

Section 32 is on the left field line near the Green Monster and is behind Loge Box 162-163.

Along with section 33, this is one of best value sections in the park. With seats priced at only $27, it is in an excellent position to view the game and the entire park. There are Loge Box seats in front of Section 32, but no Field Box seats, which makes seats in this section some of the closest to the field of any grandstand section.

Rows 1 through 7 are not affected by poles, but some seats on the right side of the section if you are facing the field are affected.

Please be aware that seats 3 through 6 in row 1 are often affected by wheelchair seating in front of them.

The view from the center of Section 32

Section 32

ROW
ROW
exit
ramp
home plate
wheelchair seating
= View of home plate or pitcher's mound is obstructed
*The view from Row 1, Seats 3 - 6 may be obstructed by the wheelchair seating

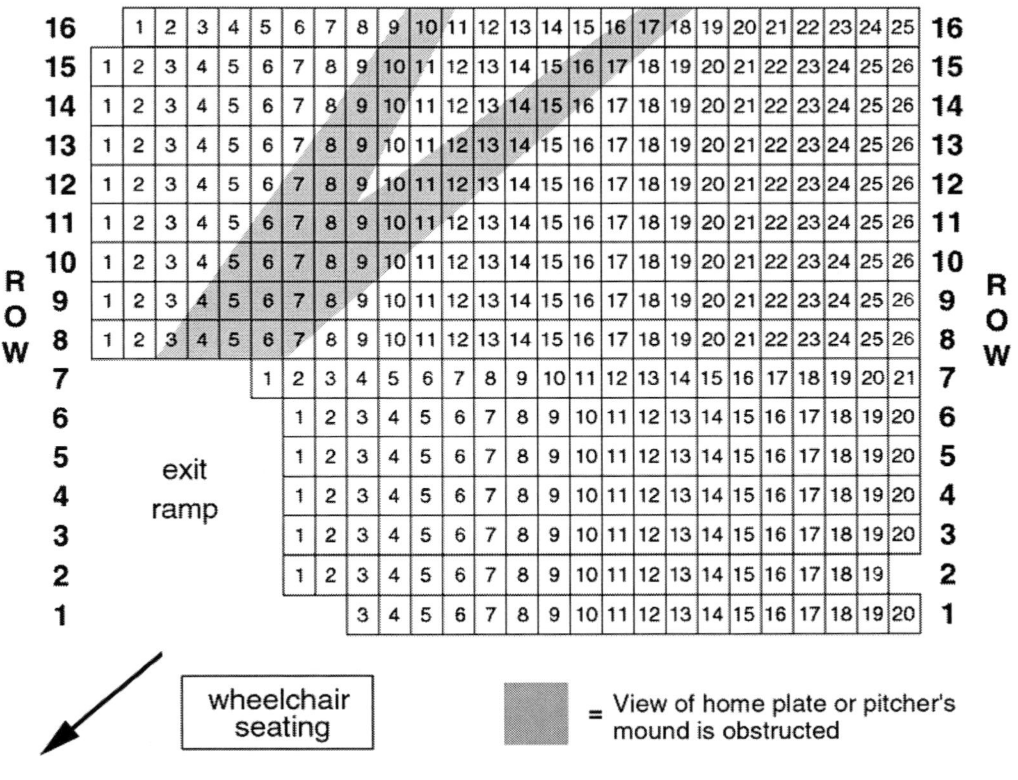

Section 33

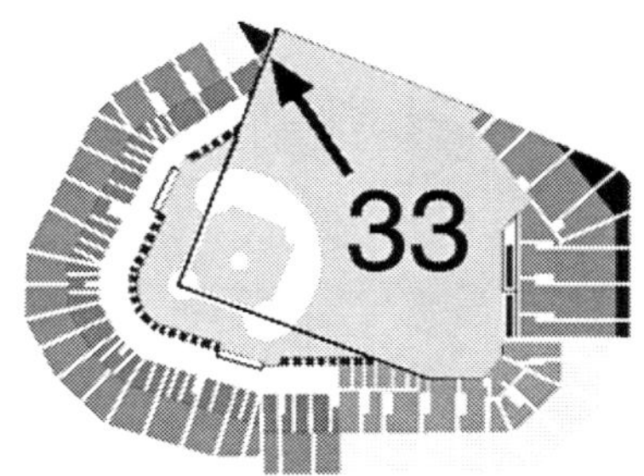

Outfield Grandstand
Face Value of tickets is $27
No alcohol section

Section 33 is down the left field line directly adjacent to the Green Monster and behind Loge Box 163.

33 is a triangular treasure tucked into the left field corner next to the Monster. It is the only Grandstand section not covered by a roof. It is the closest Grandstand section to the field, with only 1 to 3 rows of Loge Box seats in front of it. And, if you sit in row 3, seat 16, you can actually touch the Monster and the left field foul pole from your seat. This is the same pole off which Pudge Fisk hit his classic 1975 World Series home run.

Pole issues in this section run across the middle rows. If you have any seats in the first three rows you have no pole issues.

The view from the center of Section 33

Section 33

ROW
left field
foul pole
Green Monster
home plate
= View of home plate or pitcher's mound is obstructed

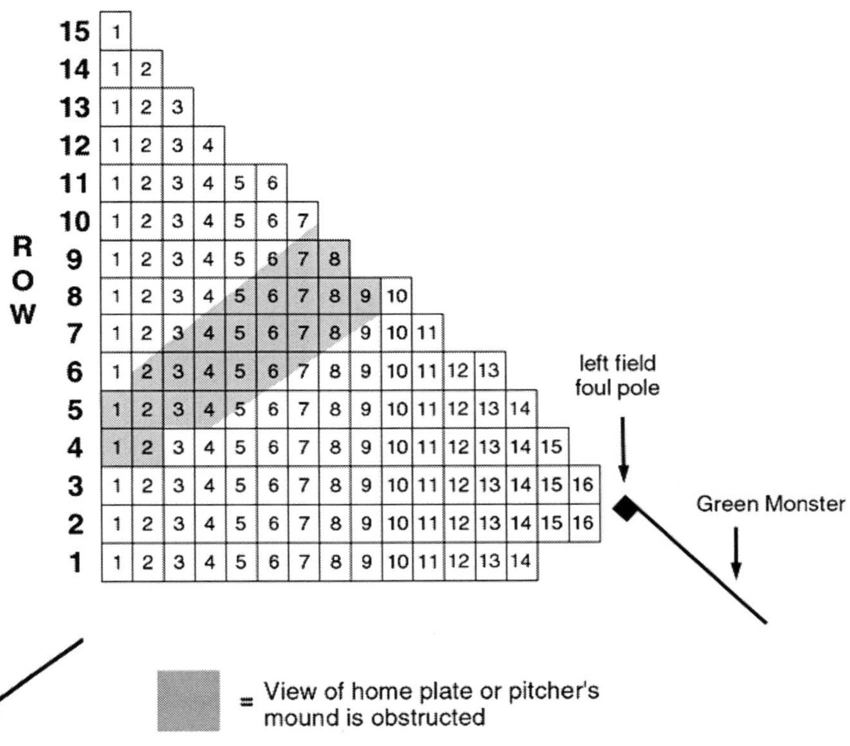

Notes